Are you in the midst of a family crisis?

Emergency Help: 911
Call 911 immediately if you are, in this moment, in danger, in deep despair, or contemplating harmful actions that will have life-altering consequences for you or someone else. Following are some additional resources to help you:

National Suicide Prevention Hotline: 1-800-273-8255
From www.suicidepreventionlifeline.org: "The National Suicide Prevention Lifeline is a national network of local crisis centers that provides free and confidential emotional support to people in suicidal crisis or emotional distress 24 hours a day, 7 days a week."

National Domestic Violence Hotline: 1-800-799-7233
From www.thehotline.org: "Our highly-trained advocates are available 24/7 to talk confidentially with anyone experiencing domestic violence, seeking resources or information, or questioning unhealthy aspects of their relationship."

Community Service Helpline: 211
Call 211 if your family crisis is not in an emergency state and is related to some form of addiction, mental health, or if you need other community services but don't know where to call. You will be referred to a local community support service. From www.211.org: "2-1-1 is a free and confidential service that helps people across North America find the local resources they need. We're here for you 24 hours a day, 7 days a week."

Call a professional. Seek help from a doctor, professional counselor, clergy, or other trusted professional or friend.

This book contains accurate information from the authors regarding their own experience, but should not be considered to be professional advice given from either the authors or the publisher. The details of every situation are different; individuals in the midst of family or personal crisis should seek the services of a competent professional, as the authors have done.

You are not alone.

WHAT OTHERS ARE SAYING ABOUT
IT'S HIS SHOW

"I am reading it a second time and have shared it with a friend...so good!"

Marilyn OShea

"Colleen and Chris's story is raw, real, and resonates with so many families struggling to find their way back to a Christ-centered foundation. I loved the book."

Patty Sears

"Wow!! What a great read...I plan to share with a good friend of mine who is struggling with his marriage right now. My absolute favorite part of the book was 'If God is in it, things can be different. If God is in it, it's worth fighting for'...truly amazing and uplifting literature."

Shawn Garmon

"...beautifully and well thought out...This book definitely lays out a path that others can follow to do the necessary work."

Vicki Hartlage

"Your book made me look at things in a whole new way... It softened my heart in how I will now look at others when their human faults and the devil's grip has a hold of them."

M B Dittmer

IT'S HIS SHOW

ABOUT THE AUTHORS

Chris and Colleen McKain were married on October 12, 1985, soon after high school. Over the next twenty-plus years, their family grew to include three God-fearing sons, each of whom grew up and married strong Christian women.

To friends at church and in the community, the McKains seemed to "have it all together." They ran a successful construction business, were involved in leading Bible studies and other ministries at church and throughout the community, were the picture of health, and by all appearances seemed happy and fully committed to the Lord, their marriage and family.

From the inside, though, their relationship was in trouble. After more than twenty years of marriage, many issues had begun eroding their foundation, warring against their hearts, sliding in-between them, unnoticed by all.

What happened next was a common story played out in home after home, every day, throughout America. When marriage gets hard, you cut your losses and start over, right?

BUT THIS IS A STORY ABOUT REDEMPTION;
ABOUT FINDING GRACE IN THE WAKE OF INFIDELITY.
THIS IS A STORY ABOUT GOD.

Learn more about the McKains today.
Visit www.itshisshow.com
Follow them at www.facebook.com/itshisshow/

ABOUT THE BOOK

It's His Show chronicles with painful honesty and wry humor the path that led the McKains to the darkest period of their lives, and the amazing and majestic power of God that brought them through it—together.

Written from Colleen's perspective with revealing insights from Chris, It's His Show pulls no punches in its raw, humble, and courageous journey through the reality of marital infidelity in Christian homes. This is not a tell–all book. Nor is it just a cautionary tale, or a feel-good story, or even a counseling process. Regardless of where you are in your marriage, It's His Show may just reveal to you some truths about your own foundation, or point you in the direction of health, of restoration, of the fullness and richness everyone hopes for in their relationship, not just with each other, but with God Himself.

For those individuals or groups who wish to go deeper, It's His Show offers a study guide suitable for individuals, counselors, or small group discussion, detailed at the end of the book.

WHY WAS THIS BOOK WRITTEN?

Through the up-and-down journey of their marriage, Chris and Colleen McKain have learned to trust God more fully. It is their desire that God would use their faith and failures to point others to the One True God who is always faithful and never fails. AFTER ALL, IT'S HIS SHOW!

COLLEEN AND CHRIS McKAIN

IT'S HIS SHOW

FINDING GRACE IN THE WAKE OF INFIDELITY

Library of Congress Control Number 2017942126
Cataloguing data:
Colleen McKain, Chris McKain
It's His Show: Finding Grace in the Wake of Infidelity
ISBN 978-0-9985592-1-6 (paperback ed.)
ISBN 978-0-9985592-2-3 (hardcover ed.)
ISBN 978-0-9985592-3-0 (Study Guide)

1. Christian Life: Love and Marriage; Family and Relationships
2. Marriage; Religion: Christian Ministry

Unless otherwise noted, all scripture references are taken from the Holy Bible, New International Version®, NIV®. Copyright © 1973, 1978, 1984, 2011 by Biblica, Inc.™ Used by permission of Zondervan. All rights reserved worldwide. www.zondervan.com Scripture quotations marked (ESV) are from *The Holy Bible, English Standard Version®*, copyright © 2001 by Crossway Bibles, a publishing ministry of Good News Publishers. Used by permission. All rights reserved. Scripture quotations marked (NLT) are taken from the *Holy Bible, New Living Translation*, copyright © 1996, 2004, 2007, 2013, 2015, by Tyndale House Foundation, used by permission of Tyndale House Publishers, Inc., Carol Stream, Illinois 60188. All rights reserved.

The opinions expressed by the authors are not necessarily those of the publisher.

Published by Encourage Publishing, LLC
New Albany, Indiana 47150 USA
1-812-987-6148 www.encouragebooks.com

Book design by Encourage Publishing, LLC. All rights reserved.
Cover design by Rtor Maghuyop with Leslie Turner
Back cover photo by Michelle Hockman Photography
Editing and interior design by Leslie Turner

ENCOURAGE
PUBLISHING

To our boys:
To know the faith and failures of your parents
so you can know that your Heavenly Father
is always faithful and never fails.

ACKNOWLEDGMENTS

WE WANT TO thank Jesus Christ for his mighty act of redeeming our marriage, the holy covenant that he instituted. We would be lost without him. Thank you, Jesus, for the hope that only you can give.

Thank you to all of our family and friends for your support and love as we journeyed through the fire. Thank you for modeling Christ to us.

Thank you to *Community Bible Study©*, our foundation for several years in the Word of God. Your materials and format are second to none, rooting us deeply in God's Word. His Word is the key for all people to hold strong to God and live in true faith.

Thank you to *Wooded Glen Retreat and Conference Center* in Henryville, Indiana, for preparing a perfect place for us to meet face to face with the Most High God to write this book. Your comfortable facility welcomed us unconditionally.

Thank you to *Preserve the Word*, for beautifully rebinding our Bibles and burning James 5:19-20 on their new, rich leather. You were able to preserve those old pages; maintaining all of their notes, scribbles and deep history, while carefully binding them together with delicate artistry to be even more precious and strong than before. Much like what God did in our lives and marriage.

My dearest Chris, I love your new heart. As God is our witness, we are not perfect souls. Rather, perfectly matched, imperfect souls called to walk side by side through this life together. You've been walking with me all this time. I will love you forever. –*Colleen*

Colleen, thank you for being my best friend. Thank you for the overwhelming grace and forgiveness you lavished over me that motivated me to want to be a better man. Your heart of forgiveness set an example for our family and so many others to follow. I love you so. –*Chris*

Now, all glory to God, who is able to keep you from falling away and will bring you with great joy into his glorious presence without a single fault. All glory to him who alone is God, our Savior through Jesus Christ our Lord. All glory, majesty, power, and authority are his before all time, and in the present, and beyond all time! Amen.

Jude 1:24-25 (NLT)

CONTENTS

FOREWORD

FOR LOVE IS AS STRONG AS DEATH,
ITS JEALOUSY UNYIELDING AS THE GRAVE.
IT BURNS LIKE A BLAZING FIRE,
LIKE A MIGHTY FLAME.
MANY WATERS CANNOT QUENCH LOVE;
RIVERS CANNOT WASH IT AWAY.
—SONG OF SOLOMON 8:6–9A

IN READING THIS powerful account by Chris and Colleen McKain, you are embarking on a journey of personal discovery in this couple's life that can also touch your own soul deeply.

For even though this is a real-life account specific to this couple, it has universal appeal and great potential for relational and spiritual benefit. This story is about a difficult and obviously serious subject: marital infidelity and patterns of the heart that lead to vulnerability and breakdown. Nevertheless, within God's time of restoration, there are plenty of delightful and joyous episodes that the McKains tell with apt cinematic imagery applied with meaningful moments of poignant humor. It is a touching and uplifting read with wonderful impact and significance!

My first step in their journey began when Chris came alone to my counseling office. He confessed that he had been involved in four affairs that had devastated his marriage, family, and many others who knew them. In fact, the mushroom cloud of destruction appeared to be continually rising with no end in sight. Chris was separated from his wife, Colleen, who was so angry on hearing the news of his infidelity that she literally and repeatedly hit him over the head with her Bible. This was no mere metaphorical "tap on the head," as Chris suffered an actual concussion from her blows! Violence and abuse is never appropriate in marriage, nor is it advocated here. Colleen was held accountable for her actions! But the amazing thing was that Chris was no longer attempting to protect himself from her influence or continuing to live in denial. He received the blows without defending himself. Thus, counseling began with Chris alone, humiliated, and incredibly broken—finally!

God's Word tells us that as a result of *the fall*, all of us have a sinful nature that wars against our soul and what God has revealed is best for us. Without Christ, we can be our own worst enemy! When someone has an extramarital affair, the hubris we only occasionally recognize becomes painfully obvious to even the most casual observer. If the truth be known, however, most of us have experienced some sort of brokenness within our own sexuality, whether we are open enough to write about it or not: brokenness not simply in our bodies but within our minds, hearts, and relationships—in our very being.

As broken people, we must go to God through Christ, confessing our sins, repenting of wrong actions and attitudes, and seeking forgiveness and restoration with God so he can lead us in renewal and healing in relationship with others. However, there are many forces in American culture and this world that dismiss the importance of admitting our humble state and guarding our hearts against temptation. Images of illicit scenes are aimed at all of us in order to sell products that supposedly add sex appeal in an empty attempt to enhance our self-worth.

Internet sites specifically designed to help married persons have affairs have been blatantly promoted on billboards and major TV networks. The Sky Harbor Airport in Phoenix, Arizona was even propositioned (we may say) with a $10 million offer to rename that facility with the title of an infamous infidelity site.[1] The New Meadowlands Stadium received a similar offer that to their credit was rejected as Arizona had earlier done with their indecent proposal.[2]

So many have become enamored with the normalization of infidelity, that a full 74 percent of men and 68 percent women surveyed speculated that they would have an affair if they knew for certain they would not get caught.[3] Of course, certainty and infidelity are two things that rarely go together unless one is thinking of the likelihood of eventually having it come to light.

Recent statistics say that the percentage of *men* who have actually strayed in *any relationship* (not limited to marriage) is 57 percent. Women in any relationship where they said they were unfaithful came in at a not-too-distant 54 percent.[4] Fortunately, the commitment of marriage does have a major impact on a couple's faithfulness in their relationship—as it is designed to do. Unfortunately, with husband-and-wife married couples, 22 percent of men and 14 percent of women still say they have strayed from their spouse at least once.[5]

While I do not possess numbers specific to committed Christian marriage, obviously infidelity strikes at believers in Christ as well.

Therefore, what is commonly referred to as *traditional* marriage, including the vow "forsaking all others as long as you both shall live," is actually a very good and radically courageous statement to make in the presence of God and human witnesses. Such a commitment is not simply *traditional*, because it is radical to swim against the flow of our sex-saturated culture. It is also especially radical when a couple looks to restore those vows after they have been broken through unfaithfulness.

Chris and Colleen came into this process in very different places, as most couples do. However, what they did have in common was honesty about their brokenness and a cry to God to make them right when they knew they could not put the pieces back together in their strength alone.

It takes divine mending to take the jagged pieces of our lives and allow them to be molded back into something beautiful in the Master's hands. One of our pastors described a Japanese pottery style called Kintsugi, where fractures and worn pieces are actually accentuated and mended with gold to add detail and character to the damage the artistic piece had once endured. This is something like what God has done for the McKains. His divine work included helping them to be transparent and accessible to each other again. His spirit of love allowed them to be accepted by the one who matters most so that they could be vulnerable and open in their journey and recovery within the Christian community. They want God to be glorified, and not themselves!

At the beginning of his ministry, Jesus proclaimed a portion of Isaiah 61 in the synagogue of his hometown. He said that this scripture was fulfilled in him (Luke 4:21). A closer look at the words from this Old Testament prophet contains the following:

> He has sent me to bind up *the brokenhearted,* to proclaim freedom for the captives and release from darkness for the prisoners, to proclaim the year of the Lord's favor and the day of vengeance of our God, to comfort all who mourn, and provide for those who grieve in Zion—to bestow on them a *crown of beauty instead of ashes,* the oil *of gladness instead of mourning,* and a garment of *praise instead of a spirit of despair.* They will be called *oaks of righteousness, a planting of the Lord for the display of his splendor.* They will rebuild the ancient ruins and restore the places long devastated...
>
> Isaiah 61:1b–4a (italics added)

We pray that through the seeking of his will, God may plant many more "oaks of righteousness" that will grow out of the ashes for the praise of His glory!

—Jeff Gilbertson, M.Div., LMFT

INTRODUCTION

ARE YOU FAMILIAR with Dave Ramsey? He is a financial guru with an immensely popular radio talk show. On his show, Dave advises the audience how to manage their money. You may have listened to him for years, attended his conferences, or read his books. One of the cruxes of his work is to share principles that encourage and enable people to get out of debt. In fact, when listeners of the show accomplish this overwhelming task, they are invited to call in and share the news live with listeners nationwide.

I love to hear the stories people share when they call in. Some of the callers have paid off tens of thousands of dollars. Some well over $100,000. It is quite an accomplishment. After all, these folks have done what a majority of Americans can't or won't do: get out of debt. These are the victorious ones.

When someone calls the show to declare their freedom, Dave Ramsey allows them to tell their story on the air. Sometimes it's a single person, sometimes a married couple, and sometimes an entire family calls to shout it out together. Finally, at the end of their conversation, Dave asks them to count it down. He makes a really big deal about it, as he should. The moment they have worked toward and anticipated for many years has finally arrived. They take a big gulp of air so their voice will carry, and they scream, "We're debt free!" Dave follows it up immediately with a clip from the movie *Braveheart* with Mel Gibson bellowing, "Freedom!"

As a listener, you can't help but smile when you hear it. In fact, you might even be grinning as you read this now. Sometimes a laugh or tear will surface. Some listeners may clap or hoot out a congratulatory "Whoop, whoop!" The callers are not the only ones who celebrate this event, though it has affected them the most. After all, they have had to claw and scratch and sacrifice to get out of debt. But it is the highlight of the show, and the audience celebrates with them. It gives everyone hope.

Sometimes I listen to Dave Ramsey while I am driving. For me, what makes those "debt free" screams even better is when I notice that the person in the car next to me is also listening to the same show. How can I tell? At the exact moment that I hear a caller shout that they are debt free, I look at the driver in the car next to me. If a smile creeps on his face, or if he gives a belly laugh, or if he raises his fist in the air and yells a victory cry, I know that he is also listening to Dave Ramsey. That makes the celebrating even more fun.

The caller's accomplishment is great. It gives the rest of us hope. Suddenly, in that moment, we feel that we may be able to make a change also.

The debt-free scream gives hope. Hope can change our outlook. Hope can raise our expectations. Hope can turn our direction. Hope can change a life.

It is my sincere prayer that this book will give you hope. God wants his best for your life. All of our circumstances are different. All of our experiences are unique. But no matter what we face in this life, we can all have one thing in common: hope.

> Therefore, since we have been justified through faith, we have peace with God through our Lord Jesus Christ, through whom we have gained access by faith into this grace in which we now stand. And we rejoice in the *hope* of the glory of God. Not only so, but we also rejoice in our sufferings, because we know that suffering produces perseverance; perseverance, character; and character, *hope*. And *hope* does not disappoint us, because God has poured out his love into our hearts by the Holy Spirit, whom he has given us.
>
> —Romans 5:1–5 (italics added)

I

DESPICABLE ME

If I say, "I will not mention him
or speak any more in his name,"
His word is in my heart like a fire,
a fire shut up in my bones.
I am weary of holding it in;
indeed, I cannot.

JEREMIAH 20:9

IN THE 1990 film *Dances with Wolves*, Kevin Costner plays the part of a soldier who befriends a tribe of Sioux Indians. In time, as they begin to get to know him, they give him the Sioux name Dances with Wolves. During one scene, the men from the tribe are hunting buffalo together. This hunt would supply food for the entire tribe for the upcoming winter. It is a majestic scene which displays the beauty of the landscape and the magnificent buffalo fleeing from the hunters. During the hunt, a young Indian, Smiles A Lot, finds himself in grave danger as a wounded buffalo charges him and knocks him from the safety of his horse. Dances with Wolves is near enough to help the boy, but is unaware of the situation.

A great warrior, Wind in His Hair, realizes what has happened, but he is out of range and cannot help. The buffalo charges toward the boy, who is standing frozen in fear. Wind in His Hair shouts with all his might to Dances with Wolves, but the noise from the stampeding herd of buffalo drowns out his voice. Wind in His Hair continues to shout as the charging buffalo gets closer and closer to the boy. He yells over and over without being heard. Finally, Dances with Wolves hears the warrior's cries and turns to see the dire situation as the charging buffalo is rapidly nearing Smiles A Lot.

Dances with Wolves raises his rifle and fires a quick shot, but misses his target. He aims again, this time a bit more carefully. He fires another shot at the threatening buffalo, but misses again. Now, it has become evident he has only one more opportunity to stop the charging buffalo and save the life of his friend, Smiles A Lot. He deliberately tightens his legs on the sides of his horse as he sits in the saddle. He raises the elevation sites on his rifle to account for the distance, takes careful aim, squeezes the trigger, and drops the charging buffalo to a skidding halt only a few inches from the boy. After the dust settles, we see that the shot saved the life of the desperate boy.

Later that evening, after the events of the tribe's hunt, the stories of the magical shot from the rifle of Dances with Wolves begin to circulate. The tribe members continue to beg Dances with Wolves to tell and retell the story. The people are mesmerized by the dramatic story, and they are amazed at what the soldier did for one of their own. But if

Wind in His Hair had not shouted out the alarm to Dances with Wolves, the story could have ended much differently. The same story would not have been told.

Sometimes we have an urgent burning in our heart like Wind in His Hair to shout out when danger is imminent. I, too, have such a burning.

Sometimes we have a story like *Dances with Wolves* that must be told over and over. I, too, have such a story.

How was the alarm finally heard? How shall my alarm be heard?

What action was taken? How was the boy finally saved? Was my own charging buffalo stopped?

We all want to know the end of the story. We all want to hear every detail. But who will shout the alarm? Who will tell the story? Who will tell my story?

I will.

I have so much stored up in my heart about what God has done. How he restored our marriage. How he healed our hearts. How he continues to refine us. I can't hold it in any longer. It is like a fire in my heart and bones, and I must declare it to anyone who will listen (Jeremiah 20:9). If there is anyone who could realize from our story how mighty our God is, I must shout it out for them to hear. I want the world to know how great God is, that he is able, and that through him there is hope.

The ancient nation of Israel reminds me of myself in so many ways. Israel, after returning from Egypt as a nation, lived under God as their ruler and had judges to make decisions on behalf of the people. Israel was made up of twelve tribes whose sum made up the nation. The Israelites became dissatisfied with the judges and wanted kings like other nations around them. They showed themselves to be stiff-necked and consistently desired their own way: a good picture of us all. God granted their request, and Israel lived under the unified rule of three kings—Saul, David, and Solomon. The people again became restless and power hungry. As a result, the nation split. Ten tribes banded together to create the Northern Kingdom of Israel. The two remaining tribes, Judah and Benjamin, became the Southern Kingdom of Judah. Over the next several hundred years, many different kings ruled each kingdom, and then they were taken into captivity due to their disobedience to God. God kept giving mercy and grace, and they kept straying from him. Much like me. Much like you!

Jeremiah was a prophet to the Southern Kingdom of Judah. It was a hard thing to be a prophet in Judah. Prophets told the truth, and the people did not want to hear it. In the verse quoted above, Jeremiah 20:9, Jeremiah was talking to God about his woes. His woes involved the fact that God had called him to speak the truth to his people, and they continued to reject him. But the words that he was told to speak were placed in his heart and bones by God, so he couldn't hold it in. He continued to speak the truth. He continued to speak what God put in his heart. He had prophesied in the previous chapter about disaster coming upon Jerusalem just before it was overtaken by Babylon, which was the beginning of Judah's captivity. A priest, Pashhur, who was also the chief officer in God's temple, heard the prophecy and did not like it.

He had Jeremiah beaten and put in stocks. The prophet of God was punished by the priest of God. Something was very wrong with this picture. Unfortunately, injustice and hypocrisy in this nation and in God's temple was not uncommon. And unfortunately, it is not uncommon in the church of today. The problem? People are people. Fleshly. Worldly. Selfish. Prideful. But praise the Lord that he has a solution: Himself.

Jeremiah had an important message. Disaster was coming. Reading it on this side of history, we can see that everything Jeremiah prophesied came to pass, and we can nod our approval. We can agree that those people were stiff-necked and would not listen to reason, which was stated just a few verses prior in Jeremiah 19:15. Yet it is easy to see the sin of others, and miss the sin in our own lives. Through my journey with God, things that are not pretty have been revealed in my life. In fact, they are ugly, sickening, and detestable to God. What shocks me more is that God is willing to give me a fresh start every time I fall. He is our God of restoration and reconciliation. He gave numerous second, third, and fourth chances to Israel also. In fact, after their captivity in Babylon, God divinely brought them back to Israel. In this, he shows us his unending grace in his continual pursuit of Israel. He shows it to us by making a way for our sins to be covered and forgiven through Christ. What a mighty God we serve.

Too bad we don't let this truth stick in our hearts. Israel was quite passionate for God upon returning to their homeland after captivity and in rebuilding the temple and the walls around the city. But the cycle of following God closely and then following the flesh even closer continued in Israel. We too can have these spiritual cycles. Sometimes our cycles last for quite a while, and sometimes, most of the time, they are minute by minute. Paul states so wonderfully in Romans 7:14–25 that what he doesn't want to do, he does, and vice versa. "For I do not do the good I want to do, but the evil I do not want to do this I keep on doing" (Romans 7:19). Are we any better?

God has taught me that I must acknowledge my sinfulness. Not only to get back in the right relationship with God, but also so that I can forgive others and desire for them to get back in the right relationship with God. Have you, like me, ever read a passage of Scripture and had your jaw drop at how rebellious and despicable the so-called people of God were acting? It is easy to see sin in others, isn't it? But I think we could all write our own movie, *Despicable Me*.

I THINK WE COULD
ALL WRITE OUR
OWN MOVIE,
DESPICABLE ME.

In the book of Judges, the nation of Israel continued in a cycle of sin, repentance, and then obedience, only to repeat the cycle several times for hundreds of years. Doesn't that just make you sick? But why does it irk us? Oh, yes, it must be because we are saddened that they have strayed from God and we wish that they would be restored to God right away. No, I don't think we are that generous with our judgments. Maybe it is because we judge them and are bothered that they would or could fall away from God's best. Yes, I think it is the latter. We just can't believe someone else would lose their way. Why are we surprised by that? It is the human condition. Yes, we should be saddened that the world, including us, would spit in God's face, but we should not look down on the other sinners as if we are squeaky clean and a rung higher on the ladder. We should, however, plead with God to restore them and drop on our face before him begging for our own forgiveness because we are also guilty of doing some spitting of our own.

When I get even a glimpse of despicable me, just a glimpse, my capacity to forgive others enlarges. And so this story begins. Forgiveness.

2

CAN YOU KNOCK ME OUT, PLEASE?

HI, I'M BOB.
CAN YOU KNOCK ME OUT, PLEASE?
JUST HIT ME IN THE FACE.

BOB WILEY, *WHAT ABOUT BOB*

JUDGE ME NOW or judge me later, but my favorite movie in the world is *What About Bob*. Bob is a nearly paralyzed schizophrenic who finds great healing by becoming a welcome member of his psychiatrist's family; welcomed, that is, by everyone except Dr. Marvin himself. In the scene quoted above, Bob has been trying to get on a bus to Lake Winnipesaukee, New Hampshire, to meet up with his psychiatrist, who is on vacation with his family. Bob feels he desperately needs to go to see Dr. Marvin to get some help. But the journey which Bob must take to travel to Lake Winnipesaukee is a huge obstacle, as he is afraid of the closed space on the bus and the danger which it represents. After fighting an inner battle, he finally makes it on the bus with Gil, his goldfish, in a jar around his neck. This whole scene is just more than Bob can take. Once seated, he asks the man next to him to simply knock him out so he doesn't have to endure any further painful anxiety.

Do you ever feel that way? If you can just check out for a while, you can get closer to the remedy for your problems and not have to endure the journey. But that is not usually the route our lives take. When I have had to cope with a mountain of betrayal and hurt, I would have liked to have gotten to the other side without having to go through what it takes to heal. But the journey is where character is built. The journey is where we are molded. The journey is how we learn. And this journey wasn't only about the healing of a marriage, but the healing of individual hearts.

THE JOURNEY IS WHERE
WE ARE MOLDED.
THE JOURNEY IS
HOW WE LEARN.

My sister used to say that I was a very private person. This was not a productive trait to carry into my marriage, but I did. I proudly agreed with her. I could keep a secret. I took pride in not spreading everyone's business all over creation, especially when it overlapped my own business. Through many years of experience, I realized that her observation is not completely true. Yes, I may be slightly guarded and private. I may measure my words carefully from time to time. I may not overshare. But more than being private, I think the driving force behind my motives of keeping things quiet may be a little more on the ugly side. Pride. I am prideful.

How does that translate into pride? My habits of keeping my own life private, in order to not be seen as weak or imperfect, stem from pride.

In the 1995 movie *First Knight*, King Arthur has a peaceful kingdom named Camelot. After many years of war, he is able to enjoy a time of peace. He finally marries his queen, Guinevere, whom he has desired to make his wife for a long time. Tragically, she is caught exchanging a steamy kiss with one of Arthur's Knights of the Round Table, Lancelot. Though Arthur could have swept this under the rug to save face, he calls for a public hearing. If the offenders are found guilty, the penalty will be death. Capitalizing on the event when the entire kingdom is gathered for the trial, Arthur's archenemy, Maleagant, storms the city with his well-armed, motley crew, bent on killing Arthur and taking control of Camelot. He commands the king to kneel before him in front of the entire kingdom. When Arthur hesitates, Maleagant asks him if he is too proud to bow. Arthur quietly and slowly formulates his answer. You can almost see him thinking about his life, his hopes, and his dashed dreams that came to a halt when Guinevere and Lancelot chose to indifferently trample the sacredness of marriage vows.

After pausing to think through the many details in this heartbreaking situation, Arthur replies with a short, succinct, humble answer. Although he does not bow a knee to Maleagant physically, it is as if his soul bows to everyone in his presence, bowing in humiliation. With a downcast and solemn face, he says, "I have no pride left in me."

I can relate to that. Though I haven't achieved a prideless state, I can relate. Although I would like to say that I have no pride left, that is not true. But I can say I have much less pride, because much of what I took pride in is gone. And it is a good thing to have less pride. The means by which it was taken away from me was not fun, nor desirable, but nonetheless, the outcome is that I have less to puff me up. In the end, God gets all the glory and Colleen gets none, so it is worth it. It is so worth it to surrender everything and say to God, "Whatever." Whatever comes my way, I am with you, God, because you are with me. So the story will unfold.

Be warned, I do not see myself as an author, but I have a story. A story that is fire in my heart and bones that I must tell (Jeremiah 20:9). Therefore, you are going to get the raw, uncut version that comes from my gut. If you do not know me and you read this with an open heart, maybe we will have a few things in common with each other, and God will continue to change us in places where we still need to be refined.

If you know me and have any lofty impressions of me, your bubble is about to be burst. I am not okay. I have problems and issues and struggles like everyone else. If that is unacceptable to you, give this book to a friend who doesn't know me.

If you know me well enough to know what a wreck I can be, read on and it will be confirmed. All of my faults will not come as a surprise to you, dear friends!

Praise the Lord that he can use anyone. Anyone. Even me. Even you!

3

LET'S START AT THE VERY BEGINNING

...FOR ALL HAVE SINNED
AND FALL SHORT OF
THE GLORY OF GOD...

ROMANS 3:23

I WAS THE youngest of four sisters in our family. My poor dad! It is not easy for anyone to live with girls, let alone four of them, plus my mom, who makes it five. But Dad held his own pretty well. I was raised in a strong, solid home. I always knew that I was loved and valued. I was sure of that. Dad was quite strict, and we had a lot of guidelines to follow. We crossed the line many times, some of us more than others, but we knew where we stood. Being the baby of the family, my sisters are certain that the rules lightened up by the time I got to high school. I am sure they were right.

My home was a safe place. I knew that Mom and Dad were constant. That goes a long way in forming a teenager's self-worth. I was far from perfect, but content. Happy. I think I was well adjusted, although I'm sure others would challenge that statement.

Chris and I met in the fifth grade. Both of our families had moved quite a bit from place to place with the changing of our fathers' jobs up to that point. But providentially, in the same year, we both moved to the same city on the same street and were in the same class at school. We spent a lot of time together as close neighborhood friends. We continued to attend middle school and high school together, remaining consistent friends throughout. Near the end of high school, we began dating. During the late summer after we graduated, we found out that I was pregnant.

So, the scramble began. We proceeded to make plans that moved toward marriage. But first things first, we had to tell our parents. Ugh. This can't be a good conversation, right? It was a difficult thing to get up the courage to do this most gut-wrenching task. One of my sisters was still living at home with my parents and me at the time.

I didn't rush right into telling my parents. In fact, my sister had to prompt me to get this party started. Several days after telling her, she decided I couldn't procrastinate any longer. She came into my room and said we needed to go and tell them now. Right then. It was a good thing she forced the issue, or they still may not know to this day. Did I already share that I excel at keeping things private? The long hallway to the family room seemed endless that night and yet, at the same time, not nearly long enough. My parents were sitting in their usual seats, and I entered the room and said that we needed to talk. I now know, as a parent, that their hearts must have sunk at that moment, for you can usually tell when bad news is on the brink. I didn't waste any time. I think it all came out in one quick sentence. It didn't take a lot of explaining to know what happened.

Mom took a deep breath and looked at Dad. I think we all looked at Dad. Mom, my sister, and me. What was going to happen next? Would it be trouble? Yelling? Would he even speak to me? My father was not an angry man, but some things can push us to act in ways that are outside of our personality. It's amazing how much faster you can think thoughts than it takes to say them, because it was only seconds before he made his move. He got up out of his recliner, the one in which my sisters and I all used to sit on his lap, the one in which he would sit with his TV tray while eating his supper, the one that my sisters and I would often playfully tip over backward all the way to the floor with him in it. He got up, held his arms out wide and walked across the room to me. With no hesitation or scorn on his face, he hugged me. And he never brought the matter up again. That has become my impression of my Heavenly Father, an impression that looks a lot like a man on a cross with arms open wide.

HE GOT UP, HELD HIS ARMS OUT WIDE AND WALKED ACROSS THE ROOM TO ME.

Chris and I were young and naive, but with the help of family, we moved forward with a plan. We got married quickly and were blessed by Chris's brother and sister-in-law, who allowed us to live in the apartment they had in their basement. It was a rough start all the way around, but God came on the scene and turned our sin into something he could use. He began transforming our hearts, and he also gave us a beautiful son. This chain of events was an upward turning point in my spiritual walk.

I had received Christ as my Savior six years earlier, when I was in the fifth grade. That night, my oldest sister was home from college and we were reading the Bible together, joined by my two other sisters. I don't know the passage we read or what was said, but somehow I understood that I needed to ask Jesus into my heart to be the Lord of my life. I realized that I was a sinner. I went to my room when we were finished reading, and I prayed for God to wash away my sins and save me. At that moment, I was suddenly at peace with God. God gave me the strong impression that the angels in heaven were rejoicing. It seemed crazy, but I rationalized that I was a pretty good prize. (Pride starts at a young age.) However, I now know that it is a spiritual truth. Luke 15:10 says, "There is rejoicing in the presence of the angels of God over one sinner who repents." Every soul is a prize to him.

After that, I knew in my heart that I was a child of God, and for a while I read the Bible and prayed frequently. In high school, I lost myself in busyness and other priorities. My fervor for God and his ways died down to embers. I was making choices that did not honor the Lord.

God used the circumstances of my unplanned pregnancy and gave me a challenge. After all, he had my full attention. It was like I had fallen into a pit in the desert sand and could not get out. That pit represented my heart of guilt and shame, feeling as if I had let God and my family down. It represented my perceptions of the heavy judgments of others regarding the poor choices I had made in my life.

It represented my uncertainties about the future. Though I could attempt to climb out, it would be in vain. The sand would continue to trickle under my weight, making it more and more difficult to climb out on my own. In my desperate state, all I knew was that I needed help. I needed God. I told him so, and he pulled me up out of my desperate pit.

Now that I was out of the pit with the assurance that God was walking with me, he drew a line in the sand. He didn't only want to save me from my current pit, he wanted my heart forever. He said, "Now is the time for you to decide what you are going to do with me." And I jumped over the line with my whole being into his open arms. I was on God's side of the line, and I wanted to stay there.

After we got married, I was introduced to a new way of thinking. Chris's family had a different way of living out their faith from anyone I had been around before. They prayed consistently before meals and seemed like "Holy Rollers" to me. They talked about God frequently. At that time in my life, I had a hard time even vocalizing the word "God." It just seemed weird. They spoke openly about what God was doing in their life. They served him completely. They appeared to have a genuine love for the Lord. It got my attention.

My mother-in-law, Dodie, took me to Bible studies right from the start. I went to Kay Arthur Precept studies with her every week, which proved to be very deep and intense. The ladies at the Bible study welcomed both me and my new baby with open arms. I saw in them a caring, accepting attitude, not one of judgment, the fear of which was heavy on my heart at the time because of my sin. God showed me that this Christian life was a good thing. And he planted a seed in my heart for loving and honoring his word.

I know that to others my growth may have seemed slow, but God challenged me with changes to make, one small step at a time. My heart belonged to him. I wanted to live for God and raise our family in his ways. God was able to get a hold of my life through my rebellious sin. God has a way of doing that. I felt as if God claimed my soul.

I believe that God can use any circumstance for his good. God never wastes a hurt. Satan may have intended to harm me, but God intended to use it for good. Over the course of several chapters in Genesis, we are told a story about twelve brothers whose descendants eventually became the twelve tribes of Israel. One of the brothers, Joseph, was envied by his brothers. They betrayed him, sold him to passing merchants, and Joseph became a slave in Egypt. Though this betrayal could have made him bitter, he remained true to his godly character. Eventually, because of God's favor, Joseph emerged as a leader in Egypt and was given a high level of responsibility. In fact, through Joseph's God-given wise counsel, Egypt stockpiled mass amounts of food before a seven-year famine, which affected the entire surrounding area. When the famine hit, Egypt controlled the food supply, and people traveled great distances to purchase the food that Joseph had gathered.

Years later, Joseph's very own brothers were driven to Egypt as a result of the severe famine. Little did his brothers know, the person from whom they were begging for food was Joseph. An ironic and surprising turn of events. The brothers finally came to a point of asking Joseph to forgive them for their grievous sin. Joseph himself offered them comfort and said, "Am I in the place of God? You intended to harm me, but God intended it for good to accomplish what is now being done" (Genesis 50:19b–20). God has a way to redeem the destruction we create.

GOD HAS A WAY TO REDEEM THE DESTRUCTION WE CREATE.

God indeed was able to use our imperfect circumstances and make them beautiful. After all, we now had the blessing of a son in our life. And a short time later, we had two more sons. With a house full of boys, our home was full of action. I loved our life, raising the boys and enjoying family. Of course, we had our ups and downs, but all in all, we had a great life. Chris was strong in his resolve for the Lord. His goal, and mine, was to keep Christ at the center of our home. Looking back, we both agree that we had a near perfect marriage. Maybe that is how pride became such a stronghold, since we wanted to protect the image that had been so real to us. Maybe that is why when it became so terribly imperfect, we were able to go through the motions and even convince ourselves that everything was as it should be.

But it wasn't. Of course, we all carry some baggage into our marriages. Obviously, some of our baggage was that we had sex before we were married. Yes, even when you marry the person you are having sex with, it is sex outside the marriage bed. It is unholy and carries consequences. Also, we both had been sexually active before we began dating each other. And Chris had dabbled in pornography at an early age. All of this added up to a slew of baggage that lessened the marriage vow. We were both guilty of polluting our purity.

And we continued to be imperfect people after we were married. Let's face it, that is why we all need to take vows at the wedding ceremony. If we weren't going to face bad times along with the good times, we wouldn't have to commit to stick it out through them. It is really a sad thing that most of us are naive about what marriage really is. Barbie and Ken always worked it out. Ken was always generous, loving, and kind, and Barbie was always more than attentive, respectful, and looked like…Barbie. So we plan our perfect weddings and think that the bliss will continue without challenges.

We aren't even opposed to marital spats in which we can kiss and make up afterward. Those are actually quite gratifying. We get to say what's on our mind, make some progress, and move forward. But the real tough stuff is when our spouse has some personal difficulty. We don't mind a disagreement or difference of opinions, but when our spouse has a real issue, a real heart issue that requires a load of hard work to overcome, we are offended and want to run away.

We have acceptable sins that we are willing to deal with in marriage, yet there are some sins that we are unwilling to cope with. We like to talk the "holy" talk that says everyone is a sinner. We quote Romans 3:23, which says that *everyone* is a sinner, because it makes us a part of "the club"; somehow we do not feel so bad about our own sin. But when our spouse sins, we say, "How could he sin against me?" "I deserve better." "He made a covenant with me." All true and valid. True and valid. But ultimately the sin is against God, and his desire is to restore the sinner. Who has the most right to be offended by a sin but God alone?

Romans 5:8 tells us, "While we were still sinners, Christ died for us." He didn't wait for us to get cleaned up. He knew mankind was sinning and that we would continue to sin. Ouch. He knew that we would spit in his face, beat him, and put a crown of thorns on his head and nails in his hands and feet every day. If he knew that and still died for us, he must be pretty serious about redeeming us and restoring us. He didn't do it because he loves to be spit on. He didn't do it because he loves to be humiliated. He did it because he loves us and wants us to have a Spirit-filled life on earth and eternal life with him. He did it for you. He did it for me. But he also did it for the person that you may not want to forgive right now. He didn't pick and choose, and say, "I died to forgive everyone except…" But do we have a tendency to pick and choose?

What drives us in marriage? What drives us in life? Is it to lift up Jesus or to lift up ourselves? A marriage is a union of two sinners walking together, hopefully with the mission of pointing the other to Christ. You may not be too thrilled at times about the person you "have to" walk next to; this is true of any relationship. Get over your lofty opinion of what you think others should be and look at yourself. You are a sinner walking with sinners around you. Did you ever stop to think that sometimes they might not be too thrilled walking next to you either?

4

UPSIDE DOWN

"You turn things upside down,
as if the potter were thought
to be like the clay..."

Isaiah 29:16

IN ABOUT OUR twentieth year of marriage, things began
to change. Who knows why we change in certain ways?
Why can't we just stay in our happy place?

For starters, we would become stagnant. This chain of
events made sure that we were not stagnant.

Our hearts, filled up with self, began hardening toward
each other. Some life events put stress on the marriage.
Within a span of three years, my dad died, Chris's mom
died, Chris went through two job changes, and our oldest
son got married, which changed our family dynamic. The
combination of these events seemed to hit Chris a little
harder than me. Tension mounted and became obvious.
In the past, we had very few harsh words with each other.
Now, they rolled off the tongue with ease. We got on each

other's nerves more frequently. Simple kindness flew out the window. Preferring one another was not on the radar. We had separate interests and liked it that way. I began challenging him in front of the kids. That didn't work well since one of the most important things men crave from their wives is respect. I did not convey respect, but blatant disrespect. I thought my ways were best. I couldn't understand why he rejected my insightful help. Our hearts were spiraling downward and hardening more and more each day.

In Mark 10:2–9, Jesus had a conversation with some Pharisees who were trying to test him. They asked about divorce, and Jesus brought light to their test by asking them what Moses said about divorce, knowing that they knew full well Moses had allowed it. Jesus made it clear that the only reason Moses gave that allowance was because of hardness of heart. In fact, in his answer, he said *your* hearts were hard, pointing the finger back at them. My point here is not to thoroughly explain when a person may be justified to divorce, for that is not the aim of this book. My point is that hardness of heart is a poison. It is so poisonous, in fact, that Moses was forced to allow them to divorce because if it. Hardness is a hidden entrance by which other sins and issues may enter, any of which may lead to divorce. A relationship that harbors hardness is ripe to be infiltrated by additional sins and become broken.

After all, if our heart is hard, we are not soft and supple in order for God to mold us. Isaiah 64:8 states, "Yet, O Lord, you are our Father. We are the clay, you are the potter; we are all the work of your hand." A skilled potter can work with soft clay to create a beautiful and useful vessel. But if any hardness begins to develop in the clay, it becomes more difficult for the potter to mold it into the desired vessel. Clay that is hardened is not in the state in which it can be molded. The opportunity is gone unless it is softened.

It is similar with our hearts. Just like the clay, if hardness of heart develops, God cannot mold us into the vessels of his choosing. We become hardened into vessels of our own choosing, which usually leads to the path of destruction. The vessels we shape ourselves into are never God's best for us.

In Isaiah 64:8, we are willing blobs of clay who recognize that he is our Father and has the right to mold us. We are nothing without him. A verse in Job tells us how valuable the process and its desired outcome is, "But he knows the way that I take; when he has tested me, I will come forth as gold" (Job 23:10). Gold? Yes. If we could see the value of the outcome, would we be willing to go through the process?

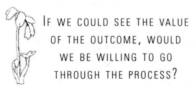

IF WE COULD SEE THE VALUE OF THE OUTCOME, WOULD WE BE WILLING TO GO THROUGH THE PROCESS?

To the contrary, in Isaiah 29:16, God speaks to some rebellious blobs of clay: "You turn things upside down, as if the potter were thought to be like the clay! Shall what is formed say the one who formed it, 'You did not make me'? Can the pot say of the potter, 'You know nothing'?" The Lord says that we have turned the example of the potter and the clay literally upside down, as if we think we are the potter. We do think that, don't we? When we disregard who he is and what he is capable of, we are saying we are the potter. When we choose to do our own thing, we are saying that we are the potter. When we look down on others and puff ourselves up, we are saying that we are the potter. When we allow the world or our flesh to harden us, we have become the potter. We are satisfied with our current ugly state and have hardened ourselves into that position. We know what is best. We are in charge of our own lives.

I have had a hard heart at times. We all have. Through the events that occurred during this time of our life, Chris's heart became more and more hardened toward God. The enemy was using it for his purposes. Chris was not in the same place with God that he used to be. I was alarmed by his hardness which began playing out in our relationship. I began to see it in his relationships with others.

I remembered Chris sharing with me about a difficult disagreement he had with some acquaintances. "I'm a hard man," he'd told me at the time. I was hopeful that Chris would recognize the accelerating hardness that had crept into his heart. Yet his shallow recognition of sin brought no lasting change. Chris was being molded into a skewed vessel. A vessel forged of Chris's flesh without the Master Potter's talented hands.

5

SERIOUSLY?

*"...*I WILL RESTORE TO YOU THE YEARS
THAT THE SWARMING LOCUST HAS EATEN..."

JOEL 2:25 (ESV)

WHILE ATTENDING A class in our new church, we were asked to write a short summary of our relationship with God and what brought us to the church. Chris and I both did this and included the challenges that we had recently faced in our marriage. We wrote our testimonies separately, but they turned out to be nearly identical. Over the next few chapters, I will include some excerpts from the testimony that Chris wrote.

A WORD FROM CHRIS

Our story is one of intense healing after having walked through the roughest time of our entire lives. My wife, Colleen, and I have been married for twenty-seven years. We have three married sons and five grandchildren. We have both been Christians since grade school. We have served the Lord throughout our marriage.

But on July 1, 2012, circumstances dictated that I needed to confess to my family that over the past four years, I had been involved in four different affairs. This nearly destroyed our family and our marriage. My wife and I separated due to my sinful habits. It was the lowest point of my life. I had taken for granted everything in my life that was so important to God and to me.

SUFFICE IT TO say, I had intense reactions to this news. Advisedly, I will not share the ugliness that came from my heart. Ugliness matched ugliness. My closest friends would not have recognized me in my moments of raw anger. On the day he confessed to our family, only the two most recent affairs came to light for me. I already knew about the first two affairs, and we had dealt with them privately. Apparently, they had not been dealt with well enough.

The first of the four affairs was not what would be called a full-blown affair by the world's definitions or standards, but to God, it was full blown. To me, it was full blown. In fact, I thought Chris had blown up our whole lives. His hardness of heart caused him to take his eyes off of what he knew to be true and right and to do what he wanted. He became his own potter. He was a believer in the Lord, but was moving farther and farther from the light, making it harder to see the correct path. He molded his life to be what he wanted it to be. He saw an opportunity and seized it.

It ended almost as quickly as it started, and with mutual resolve, we achieved a degree of healing. We pledged to make this thing work, mostly through personal determination and with only our own feeble strength. I did not want our children to find out about this because I didn't want them to be hurt. So we kept it quiet. This seems to be the norm as people try to muddle through this uncharted ground. Recovering from an affair does not need to include a public announcement, but we made the mistake of not seeking a Godly counselor to guide us through this very difficult time and into complete healing. I told no one. Remember, I'm private (or prideful, to be honest). I did not tell one soul.

As we continued an attempt at healing, we tried to help each other through the pain. Although we did not have a counselor, we talked through every imaginable aspect of the affair. Chris was truly broken, but neither of us was thoroughly healed. For the first year or so after the affair, we had countless outbursts of blame and shame exchanges. I knew I had forgiven him, but I continued to struggle with understanding, which led to anger. Chris said he felt I had forgiven him, and he knew that God had forgiven him. But the deepest hole for him was that he could not forgive himself. An affair was not something he ever planned to do. An affair was something he thought he would *never* do. He was ashamed and broken, but he did not reach out for help. We chose to invest in each other and move toward the strong relationship we once had. In fact, we got to the point where I felt that we were even stronger than before. We spent two and a half years purposefully focusing on one another.

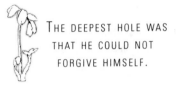

THE DEEPEST HOLE WAS
THAT HE COULD NOT
FORGIVE HIMSELF.

But one big thing got missed. A sleeping giant had been awakened two and a half years before. Generally, a person does not just get over a heightened adrenaline rush such as an affair without some serious, deliberate steps. There can be a strong draw to go back to it unless there is a determined plan of action to avoid it, and a renewed heart. I was unaware that without help in this area, he may be at a higher risk than he had been in the past, even though he knew all of the pain it had caused.

I never would have dreamt that Chris would ever do this again. The pain for both of us had been deep, but that pain is not a deterrent when you are your own potter. Although he would not want to hurt me or sin against God, the draw to please self trumps all of that when you are dealing with a stronghold that you have not addressed or admitted—or are actively trying to escape. So a woman entered the scene who had a self-made reason to make herself more than available, and he walked in with his eyes wide open. Affair number two. They told each other lies, and in the end, both knew they were using each other for the temporary.

It always floors me when someone is surprised that a person who is willing to cheat with them would not also be capable of lying to them. It is a ploy of Satan to make us feel that we are the exception. If someone wants to have an affair with you, you are not special to them; you are being used. Whether being used for physical or emotional satisfaction, it is the same. One reason is not more unholy than another. People can say anything they want in order to further their cause, and they may not even be aware that it is an outright lie. Consider the state of their heart. Their heart is at a place of moral weakness to have an affair to begin with. Their heart is divided. Their heart's view of right and wrong is clouded. Their heart is in willful sin. Why would speaking the truth be in the equation?

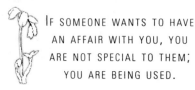

IF SOMEONE WANTS TO HAVE AN AFFAIR WITH YOU, YOU ARE NOT SPECIAL TO THEM; YOU ARE BEING USED.

I have another observation. Take it or leave it, but my observation relates to two souls whose hard hearts are ripe to fall into adultery. A man sees an opportunity (one who has made herself available) and then comes up with a reason which allows him to follow through (justification in his own mind). A woman feels she has a reason (justification in her own mind) and then creates an opportunity to make it happen (by making herself available). The vulnerable girl puts herself out there, and the vulnerable guy notices. It's a perfect match, Satan would say.

This is supported in Chapters 5 through 7 of Proverbs in which the author is warning a man to be on guard against an adulterous woman. She is making herself available because she has a self-imposed reason, such as past hurts, present challenges, or poor role models. He, on the other hand, is taken in very easily. Gullible, some would say. He may not have had a "reason" to have an affair before he saw her, but he sure can come up with a reason pretty quickly. So he needs to be warned not to fall for it. Women need to be warned to not be the adulterous woman described in Proverbs 5 through 7. Women are also challenged with this in the New Testament, which calls us to lead godly lives and to act appropriately and in modesty. A modest woman is called to not make herself available by her actions, words, and body language (1 Timothy 2:9).

Both parties involved in the adultery are equally to blame. Both sides are completely in the wrong. If one party finds a need to place more of the blame on the other party, perhaps they should stay out of situations where there is any blame to be handed out.

God used these observations and brought me to an understanding about the vows Chris and I made on our wedding day. The only people who had made vows that day in our marriage were Chris and I. We made vows to each other in the presence of God. Sure, I would love for people to honor all of the marriage vows ever made in the world, but that is not reality. I would like for the world to honor God, but it does not. The truth is that Chris was the only one who had made a vow to me. No one else had. So despite my desires for all women to keep their hands off my husband, he was the only one who promised that he would be faithful to me. And he hadn't been. Though the other women sinned, they never promised to be true to me. I can't blame them. If anyone's tail needed to be kicked by me, it was Chris's and Chris's alone.

When I found out about the second affair, I was shocked and devastated. How could he do this again? After all we had been through? After I stood beside him? There was a lot going on in his heart of which I was unaware. He also did not have complete understanding of it all. Still, the affair began and ended. We fought like cats and dogs. I protected the kids above all else by keeping it quiet. He went through the same regret and worthless feelings any person goes through who is acting in ways they wish they wouldn't. Again, we got some healing. I was still unaware of the strength of the dogs that were at war inside of Chris. Neither of us were fully educated about the power of this type of stronghold.

But I made a promise to myself: if he does this again, I will either shoot him or leave him. I was leaning toward needing a good .38 Special.

A short time later, he got involved with two different women, affairs number three and four. He had a stronghold that required all hell to break loose in order to conquer it. And it broke loose. The final two affairs came to light. Everything was coming to light. In the past, I had hoped that my prayers and all of my efforts would be enough to get us through, as if I had some superpowers. It is now confirmed—I do not have superpowers.

Having gone through this before, keeping the faith through the past two affairs that our marriage would survive, on July 1, 2012, I kicked him out.

To me, someone who would do this again after I had poured my life into trying to hold it together with every fiber of my being was history. History, I say.

Well, maybe I should do a spell check. I should have typed "*his* story." Yes, Chris and I were about to become his story. God's story.

6

GOOD RIDDANCE

A WORD FROM CHRIS

I hit rock bottom on that day, the day I had to pack my things and move out as my entire family watched me walk out of the house. I was devastated. My family was in shambles. Our future seemed hopeless. Our marriage seemed to be over.

THE FIRST DAY of July, 2012, was a bad day. My repeated hopes and dreams had been dashed. The only good news was that everyone now knew and there was no more hiding the truth. Yes, I said good news. True, it was painful for our dirty laundry to be aired to all, but on the other hand, it was cleansing. It was good to not have to deal with the secrets of covering things up. That is where true healing begins.

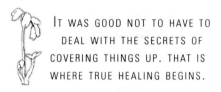

IT WAS GOOD NOT TO HAVE TO
DEAL WITH THE SECRETS OF
COVERING THINGS UP. THAT IS
WHERE TRUE HEALING BEGINS.

All of our kids were gathered at the house as usual that Sunday afternoon. Chris confessed to the entire family what had been happening in his life for the past few years. They witnessed Chris gather up his things and head out the door with his suitcase. Good riddance, I always say. In the words of Truman in the 1998 movie *The Truman Show*, "Oh, and in case I don't see you, good afternoon, good evening, and goodnight."

Our kids were shocked, crushed, upset, and yet so very tender with both of us. We have amazing kids. They stayed with me all that day and continued to check on me and care for me. They each had their own time frame for dealing with Chris, and that was good. Everyone who was affected by this had their own way of dealing with it and responding to it.

Later that same evening, some close friends of mine came over to listen and pray with me. I was exhausted by the events of the day; I told them that they didn't need to come, but they didn't care what I said. They made the right choice to ignore my wishes. I will never forget them sitting with me and sharing my sorrows. They listened and asked gentle questions. They spoke very little and prayed with me. After not breathing a word to a soul for four years, I was especially grateful when I finally could speak openly, share my hurts, and get some encouragement. One of them said words that rang true in my head, words that opened the door for me to think that maybe, and that's a big maybe, this wasn't the end. "God can do what man says can't be done." Was it possible?

In the moments immediately after the big reveal, I was absolutely, 100 percent, no holds barred, completely finished with our marriage. I could hear a song ringing in my ears, the song that the coroner in *The Wizard of Oz* sang about the Wicked Witch of the East, but this time it was about my marriage. "As coroner I must report, I have thoroughly examined it, and it's not only merely dead, it's really most sincerely dead." But the power of a covenant is amazing. As I went to bed that night, God placed a powerful truth on my heart. He wanted us to stay married. I began to ponder the idea, and we were only hours into this thing. I believe that any marriage that can be saved should be saved. Though I had strong doubts that it could work, I felt that God may be on to something. Eventually, I surrendered to the fact that I made a covenant and I was going to keep it.

I MADE A COVENANT AND
I WAS GOING TO KEEP IT.

Chris and I texted a few times that evening. I did not share with Chris my impression from God. I still had plenty of venting to do, and God had plenty of surgery to do. Chris was recovering from the shock of all that had transpired so quickly. God was putting on his surgical gloves. God was scheduled to perform an extended and deliberate, sometimes gruesome, surgery on Chris's heart.

That kind of stuff usually makes me queasy, but I rather enjoyed watching this surgery.

Earlier on that same Sunday morning, before any of this came to light, I felt God nudging my heart to pray for Chris. God had given me a similar impression two times in the past, each just before I became aware of the first two affairs. At this point, I thought I was just feeling the effects of Chris's divided, hard heart and entanglement in sin. It poured over into our relationship even though he was making generous attempts to hide it.

That morning, still unaware of his most recent two affairs, I felt that I should pray for his love for God to be rejuvenated. I had been praying for him for years, and quite frankly, I was tired of it. I reluctantly share with you that in the recent past I had been saying to God, "If this is all you are going to do in Chris, then this is all I'm going to do. Apparently, you are not going to answer any of my prayers, so I'm done." I felt God saying that he had not given up on me or Chris. He was preparing my heart to accept what he was about to do. I felt God rebuking me for pulling away from him because I was not getting my way in my time. But I still harbored the reality that I had prayed for years and expected some results. Where were these results, God?

The impression that I got was clear. It was almost an audible voice from God. "Do not give up. I am going to show you something more powerful than you have ever seen. I am going to change a heart." What? Yeah, right. Like you have done in the past with his heart? Okay, God. I'm watching. I'm watching. I guess this is your show. And just when my clenched teeth and sassy mouth spouted off to God, I happened to read 1 Samuel 12:16, "Now then, stand still and see this great thing the Lord is about to do before your eyes!" "All right, God. I'm watching." And as time passed, God kept whispering in my ear the words of my friend, "God can do what man says can't be done."

GOD CAN DO WHAT MAN
SAYS CAN'T BE DONE.

7

BREATHE

A WORD FROM CHRIS

I spent that first night in a hotel. I didn't sleep. At least Colleen was willing to text with me. Even though the texts were not pleasant, we were talking. God had to do a tremendous work in my heart for our marriage to be saved. I prayed all night. I studied all night. I looked for God all night. My sin of the past had kept me from hearing from God. My prayer life and my study life had been dry bones for so long, but on the morning of July 2, God began to step in and began to answer prayers.

He miraculously provided a place for me to stay temporarily, where the host family would turn out to be instrumental in helping to save our marriage. This was one of the first of his many miracles: enabling this family to take me into their home. God was hearing me again. It was a miracle. I began to study with my friend at his house, and he was helping me find the Lord. My heart was repentant and was softening. My Bible was coming to life for me again. God wanted to have his way with my heart—I see that now, looking back. As each moment passed by, I was beginning to sense the Lord's presence more and more as he orchestrated the most intense healing of my life—our life. Our marriage needed to be healed! And it had to start with me.

GOD CONTINUED TO work on behalf of our marriage. And much help came from family and friends. On that first night in his hotel room, Chris had a dear soul come and meet with him, his oldest brother. If I was crushed, Chris was crushed, ripped, and torched. Honestly, I would much rather be in the position of the offended than the offender. I was hurt beyond belief, but he faced the guilt and sorrow of causing it all. I know that in some cases this may not be true, but having lived through it, in our case, I had the easier road.

The next day, Monday, July 2, several family members came over to our home to hang out with me under the guise of a swim party. I had a ready-made party, and I didn't have to plan anything. I decided I could really get used to this. No one let me do a thing. No one mentioned what was going on. Just being present was all that was required.

It made me think of Job's friends who came to help him when disaster struck his family. He lost all of his oxen, donkeys, sheep, camels, servants, sons, daughters, and he was even struck with painful sores from the top of his head to the soles of his feet (Job 1:13–2:10). Upon hearing the news, Job's three friends came, sympathized with him, and mourned with him (Job 2:11–12). "Then they sat on the ground with him for seven days and seven nights. No one said a word to him, because they saw how great his suffering was" (Job 2:13). This was a tremendous ministry of silence. But for the sake of my example, I will stop there and not draw attention to the fact that their visit with Job went downhill after this.

That is what my family did for me. I did not need to have conversation. Silence was fine with me. They knew that silence suited me. This was just one example of the many acts of kindness shown to me as I was trying to get my head to stop spinning.

For Chris at the hotel, Monday morning was the beginning of a story of miracles for him, miracles that would ultimately be for us both. A precious friend of ours went to visit with Chris that morning at the hotel. They were able to talk a lot, but Chris conveyed to me later that just his presence was all he needed. His friend took time to just go and be with Chris.

After his first night in the hotel, the first obstacle for Chris was where to live. Chris began thinking and praying about where he would stay. This would prove to be the first of innumerable prayers that God would answer for us during this time. God's timing is perfect. He immediately answered Chris's prayer by placing a friend's name on his mind, Kirk, a friend that Chris had not seen or spoken to in several months.

Chris immediately called Kirk and shared our story with him. Chris confessed everything to him. Kirk graciously listened, but Chris did not know what type of a response to expect. Would he want to scold Chris? Would he want to teach him a lesson? Would he hang up on him? All this and more ran through Chris's mind. Without knowing it, Kirk's response would be another step in our marriage being saved. Kirk immediately responded with a single question, "How can I help?"

Chris was silent. The tears began to flow and prevented him from speaking. He humbly replied, "I need a place to stay."

Without hesitation, Kirk offered for Chris to stay with him until he could find another place.

The timing of this whole event was another miracle that God poured out on us. Kirk's home was available for one week that summer, and it happened to be that specific week. To explain, Kirk is a coach at a local high school, and as God beautifully worked things out, that week was what is called "dead week" in Indiana. Dead week is the week when players and coaches take a break and are not allowed to practice. Coaches are not even allowed to have contact with the student athletes. So not only was Kirk's home available, but Kirk himself was available. He sacrificed his one week of vacation, which is extremely valuable to a coach in Indiana, and he selflessly made himself available. On top of that, Kirk's son sacrificed his bedroom and slept on the couch so Chris could have his own room, a quiet place.

Kirk is a godly man who pulled up alongside Chris. He counseled him all week, listened to Chris, prayed with him, and encouraged him. Kirk gave Chris relevant articles and provided constant wisdom. He prepared pertinent Bible studies that they did together every morning. Kirk knew there was only one source of healing for Chris: God's Word. And he was right. Chris was being transformed by God's Word, which had been dead to him for so long.

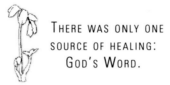

THERE WAS ONLY ONE
SOURCE OF HEALING:
GOD'S WORD.

On Tuesday, July 3, during their first morning Bible study, Kirk knew that Chris was overwhelmed with pain and anguish. Even though God was the surgeon, this open heart surgery was proving to be extremely painful. Chris's pain was visibly noticeable to Kirk. Kirk quietly reached across the table for the notepad on which Chris was making notes. He pulled it to his side of the table. Kirk proceeded to write a single word, a word that still impacts Chris to this day. Tears flowed down Chris's face as he saw Kirk's pen write on the page. Kirk carefully wrote the word *breathe*.

Kirk could feel Chris's pain. He was sensitive to the fact that a fellow brother was in dire need of help. He recognized that Chris needed to start with the basics of returning to his spiritual first love. Something as simple as breathing was a huge undertaking. But by God's grace, God gave Chris each and every breath he would need to survive the surgery God was performing. Kirk's one written word put it all into perspective for Chris, and he knew he had to trust in God for everything, even each and every breath. Although it was painful, what a wonderful place to be: to rely on God for all things. Nothing taken for granted.

Every breath praiseworthy. That's how we must be when it comes to allowing God to have his way with our heart!

8

INDEPENDENCE DAY

A WORD FROM CHRIS

On Wednesday, July 4, 2012, God turned my entire life around. I believe that day is the day that I was brought back from the dead. I believe that day is truly my "Independence Day." God spoke to me in my heart and told me that I needed to purchase a new wedding ring—right then. I never wore my old ring, which was still at the house. Since I wasn't living at home, I didn't have access to it. So, I got in my truck and headed to Kohl's. While I was driving to the store to buy a ring, I noticed the Christian music on the radio had begun to come alive to me.

When I arrived at Kohl's, I quickly found the ring that I needed. I purchased it, and I sent a picture of it to Colleen. When I finished at Kohl's, I drove back to my friend's house where I was staying. I parked in the driveway alone. I literally sat in my truck for two hours as fireworks were going off all around me. The music on my radio had captivated me, and I began texting the powerful lyrics of the songs to my wife. Little did I know at the time, but the things I did that night are what gave my wife peace to want to begin to work out our marriage. She texted me, saying, "You're walking back to me." That changed my perspective on everything. All I wanted at that time was for the Lord to have his perfect way with my heart and to clean me out and to make me new. And that is what he has done. And that is what he has been doing in me every day since! His grace and redeeming power changed me and saved me on that Independence Day.

ON WEDNESDAY, JULY 4, while still at Kirk's house, Chris was drying off after taking a shower. He noticed something missing on his hand: his wedding ring. God spoke to him to immediately buy a new wedding ring. He said it was almost an audible voice, and it was urgent. When you hear from God, you better move! So he got in his truck and headed to the store. He had not worn his ring for many years, due to the nature of his work and possibly because he did not see value in it. It was not really a topic of discussion between Chris and me, but it bothered me deeply. However, I had stepped aside and taken a position of silence on certain issues in recent years. I decided to let the Holy Spirit do the convicting on this issue in our marriage. Still, the ring issue was number one on my "to do list" of things that I wanted God to talk to him about. Well, God did. God had told me he would show me great things, remember? And I was watching. And I must say, this was a great thing, without my having to say a word. Chris texted me about this encounter with God and sent me a picture of the ring on his finger. A revival was happening in Chris's heart on this day, his Independence Day.

As he drove to purchase the ring, he began listening to Christian music on the radio. For the past few years, during this time of hardness in his heart, he was not interested in Christian music on the radio. He would often criticize the music and judge the lyrics. This was another thing on my list for God to talk to him about. Actually, it was number two. You may wonder why this would be so high on my list. I think it was because it revealed his heart to me. I knew the man that I used to be married to, and this wasn't him. It bothered me that he would have such a sour attitude toward something that was good. Maybe it was difficult for him to listen to? I don't know for sure, but on this day, it was healing to his heart. It was bringing life to his dead bones.

Not only was God doing a work in Chris, but he began doing a work in me too. I loved God deeply, but honestly, I had lost a lot of hope that he would ever do anything with this wandering husband of mine. I had said many times, "God, you created him, you do something with him." I had given him over to God a while ago, dumped him at the foot of the cross and left him there. I'm pretty sure I was not doing it the way people envision when they say to leave your problems at the foot of the cross.

Every year, we would host a Fourth of July party for our family. I decided to go ahead with the party this year as planned—without Chris. But I noticed a conflict stirring in my heart. Chris was not there. He really was *not there*. Life was going on without him. This conflict really got my attention when he began texting me the lyrics to the

Christian music he was listening to. There was a barrage of texts from him that didn't stop coming for several hours during the party. It was quite a miracle to me that he would be wearing a wedding ring, listening to Christian music, and actually sending the lyrics to me. (Is that legal?) It was reminiscent of my old husband. What was God doing? I had prayed for this. God was showing me something great.

I bravely texted him back that night, "You're walking back to me." Forgiveness can be a process, and the process was beginning on Independence Day. Chris's heart was beginning to soften. My long list of things that "had to change" began getting checked off one by one. I had never revealed my list to Chris, but through God's miraculous involvement, God continued to reveal things to Chris, and Chris responded. God was showing me over and over that he was willing and able to change this man's heart, not just for me, but because God's desire was for Chris to be transformed into a useful vessel in the kingdom. These were much greater plans with a much better motivation than the list of a wife. I was not going to stand in the way of a miracle.

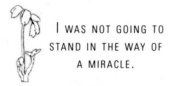

I WAS NOT GOING TO STAND IN THE WAY OF A MIRACLE.

With the changes in living arrangements and the details that surrounded it, it seemed like a lot of time had passed, but we were only in the first week of this process. That Friday, July 6, we arranged our first face-to-face meeting. It was an emotional meeting. Chris walked into the house, and we were overcome by emotion as we saw each other again. We talked and cried. We even had to laugh a little about some of the intense actions and reactions that had occurred in the past week, some of which I was not proud.

Something amazing happened that first day Chris and I saw each other. We were sitting very close on our couch talking things through. All of a sudden, Chris exclaimed that he could see me. For the past few years, his eyes had been rapidly deteriorating, and he had started wearing reading glasses. Without the glasses, things that were close up were generally quite a blur to him. He wasn't wearing his glasses at this time, and yet he was noticing every detail of my face. Normally, my face would have dissolved into a haze at that distance. That's when I realized that I should have taken more time getting ready that morning. He noticed every freckle and spot, every wrinkle and smile line. And contrary to how most women feel about people getting a close look at these "character lines", it was good that he could see them! Chris's clear vision was a miracle!

God gave Chris new eyes with which to see his bride. God was showing Chris the bride of his youth. God was showing him that his bride had aged! If Chris wasn't sure what he was signing up for, he knew now. It was as if God gave him a glimpse of his past, present, and future. It was a gift to Chris to be able to see so clearly, if only for that fleeting moment. Those clear eyes lasted only for the duration of that visit, and now his eyes are back behind the bifocals if he wants to see. But it certainly was a very powerful event to give God's seal of approval on our goal to reconcile.

Additionally, with the passing of each day, Chris also noticed a huge increase in his clarity of thinking. Without all of the sin tangling up his brain and dividing his heart, he was able to focus. He said there was so much freedom in getting all that junk out. Being double-minded makes the one brain we have very confused. James 1:8 says that those who are double-minded are unstable in all their ways. Double-mindedness clouds our thinking. Chris's heart was being cleaned up, and so was his mind. God was performing brain surgery.

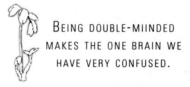

BEING DOUBLE-MIINDED MAKES THE ONE BRAIN WE HAVE VERY CONFUSED.

Throughout this process, I could see God doing a mighty work. Some of the progress I saw I kept to myself because I was soaking it in. Gathering information. I was observing. I was watching. It began to sink in that this was God's show, and I couldn't wait to see what would happen next.

9

SO THAT'S WHAT WORSHIP IS

A WORD FROM CHRIS

A friend encouraged me to attend church with him on July 8. I did, and Colleen attended with me. We were on our road to being healed. It was the most powerful service I had experienced in years because, for the first time in a long time, worship was real to me. Worship comes to life when God has saved you. I finally understood what God's grace truly is because that was all I had! And all I could think to say was "Thank you, Jesus!" The service spoke to each of us. God showed up, and he helped us that first day we attended. Jesus was there for us.

AS SUNDAY, JULY 8, approached, I knew I wanted to go to church, but where? Throughout the week, I was torn about where to attend church, especially on this first Sunday of our separation. Chris and I had been going to church together our entire married life. Our children were grown, and each attended a different church. Knowing I was alone, they each invited me to go to church with them, but I was still feeling uneasy about it. Anything that happens for the first time after a big life change can be uncomfortable, even a bit scary. And church had always been my safe place.

About midweek, Chris asked me if I would go to church with him. At first, I really could not see myself going to church with him any time soon. Just not happening. I was still in a painful place and didn't want to share such an intimate setting with Chris.

After spending the day with Chris on Friday, and knowing that my resolve was for us to be reconciled (although I had not told him yet), I decided to go to church with him on Sunday. Some precious friends had invited us to join them. It was a big church in a neighboring city "where nobody knew our name." It would have been difficult to attempt to attend any churches in our immediate area, because it would be probable that we would see people we knew who were aware of our situation. This would happen eventually, but at this point, we were both very fragile and needed to worship without additional distraction.

I still marvel that we even went to church together. It was most definitely God's doing because on the previous Sunday, in my heart, I was headed to find a good lawyer. Now, just seven short days later, we worshipped together. It was a very emotional morning, but it was so good to be in God's house. Every part of the service spoke to each of us, as you can imagine. Hearts that are raw are easily penetrated.

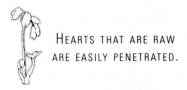

HEARTS THAT ARE RAW
ARE EASILY PENETRATED.

The sermon title was "A Kingdom Torn in Two." How's that for irony? It was a sermon from a series called "The Story," based on the book by the same name. The series took the church through the Bible from start to finish. The message that morning seemed to be just for us. It was another stepping stone for us to solidify our resolve to save this covenant that God had established.

A narrator spoke before the preacher began the sermon.

> *"If life barges in with a broken marriage, and if God redeems you through deliverance from sin and judgment and death, why? So that everything can be different. So that your mind and heart and marriage and family and job and kids can all be made new. That's the purpose of every good story. That's the purpose of God's work in you. That's new life."*

Those were perfect words for me to hear. Words of hope. Things can be different! If God is in it, things can be different. If God is in it, it's worth fighting for. It set my mind to wondering what might be different in the lives of my children and grandchildren if I chose to stick it out and make this marriage work. What might be different if I chose not to stick it out? To quote from the 2000 movie *Gladiator*, "What we do in life echoes in eternity." As far as it was up to me, I wanted the echo to bring glory to God.

The pastor preached an amazing, pertinent sermon after the narrator spoke. It was a difficult sermon for him to deliver; before he began he had to make an announcement about the church's worship leader, who had died unexpectedly the day before. Yet, through the pain, he obediently preached a sermon that made a difference in our lives, maybe an eternal difference in the lives of our children and grandchildren. He said, "The decisions that we make today and the way we live our lives will affect generations to come in either a positive or negative way."

His final thought seemed to actually be from God's heart to mine, simply using the mouth of Dave Stone: "God is not uninvolved. When people sin, God responds. When people repent, God responds. When God seems distant and just doesn't make sense, give him time. He will respond." That was a word just for me. I had been begging God to do something for years, but hadn't given him the time to work according to his own timetable, which is timeless. Apparently, though, now was the right time. This was the time that I had been praying for all those years. This was the time in which God had Chris right where he wanted him and was doing some of his best work: changing a heart. How could I deny this answer to many years of prayers and not be on board?

> *But do not forget this one thing, dear friends: with the Lord a day is like a thousand years, and a thousand years are like a day. The Lord is not slow in keeping his promise, as some understand slowness. He is patient with you, not wanting anyone to perish, but everyone to come to repentance.* 2 Peter 3:8–9

What seemed like an eternity to me was a short time in God's timetable of eternity. This analogy of one thousand years being as a day to the Lord is a simple means in which our finite minds might get a glimpse of how infinite God really is. It is not meant to be a math problem. But if it were a math problem, my years of praying were only about five minutes to God. My husband had come to repentance. That was the ultimate goal. It was worth waiting for. My resolve became even more steadfast. God was in this thing. I wouldn't miss it for the world.

Many people have asked me, "How did you do it?"

Others have confided, "I don't think I could do it."

My response is, "Yes, you could." Trust God. You can do more than you think you can. In fact, you can do anything that God calls you to do. "For I can do everything through Christ, who gives me strength" (Philippians 4:13, NLT).

In the movie *What About Bob*, Bob is invited to go sailing, and he reluctantly agrees. After determining that the craft is seaworthy, he embarks upon his first sailing experience. The movie reveals to us how he is able to overcome his fears: he ties himself to the mast with multiple life jackets strapped to his body. Is he really sailing? Does he operate the craft? Does he manipulate the sails? No. But he excitedly declares to all who could hear, "I sail!" His testimony for his success is, "I just let the boat do the work."

The same applied to me. The trick for me was to let God do the work. When his Spirit is at work within us, we are power-filled. God loves to get a hold of us when we are helpless, when we don't have an ounce of strength left. Paul says in 2 Corinthians 12:10, "For Christ's sake, I delight in my weaknesses, in insults, in hardships, in persecutions, in difficulties. For when I am weak, then I am strong." That is when God is shown mighty: when we are empty of self. He wants that surrender. He can use that surrender.

Yes, I believe everyone can do more than they think they can when they quit doing and start surrendering. The pastor preached that sermon when his flesh was at a low point of sorrow at the loss of a loved friend, but he let God do the preaching, and it was powerful. When a wife "plugs away" at a troubled marriage until she finally has nothing left to give, that's when God can take over and become her strength. A person's heart can be changed when they have no power left to change it themselves; then, the Master can finally begin his work. Whatever the situation, he will be faithful to walk with us through it all, regardless of the outcome.

We made it through our first week of healing. God still had his surgical gloves on. God made it clear; he was not only doing surgery on Chris's heart, but he was doing surgery on both of our hearts. The only thing is, in a normal heart surgery, anesthetic is administered so the patient does not have to endure the pain. No anesthetic was given here. We went through the pain full strength, and it was a big part of the learning process. Chris and I walked through the fire together.

10

TAKE OFF YOUR SHOES

A WORD FROM CHRIS

I was seeing glimmers of hope, but my heart was aching because my wife wasn't ready for me to come home any time soon, and she urged me to find an apartment. It was difficult for me to even think about looking for an apartment, much less living in one. As I was looking for an apartment, another friend called to tell me that he had a place for me to live. Another miracle from God. His mom moved out of her apartment temporarily so I could stay in her fully furnished apartment. The apartment turned out to be a place where God really spoke to me.

The time living alone provided the means that God would use for twenty-five days to meet with me and to change me. As the days passed by, our marriage grew stronger and stronger. My wife invited me to move back home on July 30, 2012. We still had much more healing to go through, but now we would do it under the same roof. Yet another miracle—the fact that my wife invited me to come home!

EVEN THOUGH WE were working on our marriage, real life went on. Chris could only stay with Kirk for one week, and then he needed to move out. I wasn't ready to have him home yet. I told him he needed to find an apartment. And God stepped in and revealed a place for him to live. God's provision.

God's miracle of provision came through Chris's friend who sat with him at the hotel on July 2. He had mentioned to his mom that Chris needed a place to stay at the end of the week. Amazingly, this precious woman chose to move out of her apartment and allow Chris to move in. This sacrifice affected her daily life. Now she would have to drive further every day to and from work. It would mean packing up the items she would need and living in a makeshift place, which is always an inconvenience. It would mean a shift in routine in the home in which she stayed. I believe that somewhere along her road, people had helped her through tough spots, and she had it on her heart to help others. She believed in God's healing. She believed in restored marriages. God was using her to help us. Her hospitality and heart of sacrifice impacted our lives because she was obedient to God. Only God could orchestrate every minute detail of the arrangements of the apartment for us.

We moved Chris into his apartment on Friday, July 6. And yes, you read correctly, I said *we*. It may seem odd that I would be a part of this move. After all, we were separated. But my approach to the separation was that, hopefully, it was temporary, and to be used for a time of individual reflection and healing. I also wanted to know every detail. I wanted to know where he had been and where he was going. I am an information gatherer, and I was harvesting every bit of data I could get my hands on in this unchartered territory.

When the apartment became available, we went to gather Chris's things from Kirk's house. Chris showed me where he had been staying, and he gave me some details about his time there. It was a beautiful thing to hear the many details about this place where God had spoken to him when he was in the deepest pit of his life.

He showed me the kitchen and the table where he and Kirk had their Bible studies that first week. As I mentioned before, Kirk spent time with him every day in God's word. This was a tremendous effort on Kirk's part to prepare and take the time to spend with Chris. He showed me the journal that he had been keeping. He had been writing his regrets, confessions, Scriptures, thoughts, and prayers to God daily. He showed me the page that contained the list of apartments which he had been calling to try to set up his new life without his family. That was the same page on which Kirk wrote that life-giving word: *breathe*. That's when I felt the desperation that had plagued Chris during that first week.

Chris showed me the bedroom where he stayed. It was decorated in sports themes and was clearly a young person's room. Chris said that it reminded him that he needed to have the faith of a child. He was starting from infancy in his walk with God. Chris told me he had heard from God in so many ways in this place. Chris reminisced about each one. I could see a difference in my husband. He had been with God! I eagerly listened to the mighty works of our mighty God. God was blessing my soul by allowing me to see, touch, and feel everything that God was doing to save Chris and our family.

There was one more room that he wanted to show me before we left this place of God's presence. I'll never forget his eagerness and excitement as he led me to the room. He led me to the bathroom. The bathroom? Yes, the bathroom. God can speak to us in any way he chooses. He can even speak to us in the bathroom.

Chris told me, "This is where I heard God's voice."

This bathroom was the place in which God stopped Chris dead in his tracks as he got out of the shower and told him to get a new wedding ring. He still wears that same ring to this day, while his old one lies on his dresser. The new one is a joy to both of us.

It meant so much to me to know every detail of how God was personally teaching and ministering to Chris. It was a privilege to have seen the place where God met with Chris so harshly and yet so tenderly that first week. After all those years of prayer, God was showing me that he was more than capable of handling the situation I had brought to his throne so many times.

We finished gathering the belongings at Kirk's and headed to Chris's new apartment. Seeing the apartment for the first time gave me peace. It was such a nice place and was set up to meet all of Chris's needs. This was his new home. He would live life there. He went to work from there, shopped for his own groceries, made his own meals, did his own laundry, kept the place clean, and had plenty of quiet time.

At first, the apartment was a hard pill to swallow for Chris. He really didn't want to stay away from home. But it needed to happen. God needed to meet with each of us individually without the pressure of constantly being together. The apartment cleared the way for us to deliberately enter a season of courting. For new habits to form. For appreciation of each other to renew. For God's will to take center stage in our lives.

As he had looked for an apartment, Chris shared with a friend the grief over being separated from his family. His friend made it clear to him that though this may be a part of the consequence of his sin, it was also something that was needed. He said that this was a time for God to get a hold of him. His friend was right. Chris needed it. I needed it.

As Chris looked back on the time in the apartment, he was amazed by the great healing that took place. There was no escaping the reality of why he was there, or the fact that God was all he had at that time. It was a time of getting back to the basics of his faith and listening to and seeking God. He was able to throw off all the distractions and focus on his relationship with God. He was able to hear clearly from God because the sin that had ruled his life for so long was finally getting cleaned out. He wanted to be healed. He began to pray as a man who was seeking, not hiding. The words of his Bible came to life in his heart again. He lovingly refers to that place as holy ground.

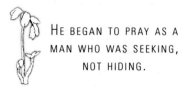

He began to pray as a
man who was seeking,
not hiding.

During the weeks of his time at the apartment, I would meet with him there. Even though I embraced the fact that distance was required, I was drawn to be a part of where the action was. God's presence was heavy in that place; I could feel it. I watched everything that was happening with great intent.

The apartment provided a fresh beginning. We were starting over. Sometimes we would schedule for me to go there, or sometimes I would surprise him and show up unannounced. We would take walks, he would cook meals for me, we would study and pray together, and we had lots of good talking time. We talked about nothing and everything. Of course, we discussed our marriage and began to work through a lot of garbage. We had many necessary conversations, healing conversations. And we also had many hard, tense conversations. More than once, Chris had to remind me that we were in an apartment building and I might want to reconsider my volume. As we muddled through the details, both hurt and healing occurred. I wanted to know every detail of the affairs, which may not be necessary for some in our situation. But for me, it was important. If this was a new beginning, we needed a clean slate with nothing hidden.

Chris spent a good part of that first month on a partial fast. At first, he did not eat because he had no appetite, but then he began to embrace the practice of denying self so he could focus fully on God and not miss anything that the Lord was communicating to him. Chris seldom had meals during our separation, but when we were together, he would eat heartily. He was only content and relaxed enough to eat when we were together.

After thirty days of separation, I invited Chris to come home. To some, this may seem like a short time. What is right for some may not be right for others. But for us, our hearts were ready to continue our healing under the same roof. Just as the separation had a time and purpose, so did the reunion. An important note is that just because a couple moves back in together, it doesn't mean that they are completely healed or that progress has ceased. You can continue to work on things while living together. Isn't that the premise of a marriage in the truest sense? In marriage, we must work through issues every day. For us, it actually added a dimension of reality, and we faced a new set of challenges which was a natural part of the process. It was progress. And God continued to do surgery on our broken hearts.

While walking with Chris through his time at Kirk's home and his time at the apartment, God had certainly piqued my interest. I had been watching everything Chris was doing, and I took in every little victory with joy. But the best part of the show was watching each and every move my Savior made. God cared so deeply for us and our covenant. He was in this thing, heart and soul. My love for the Lord was increasing with each passing day as I grew to know him in a new and fresh way. I sensed God's hand resting upon me. It was as if he was literally touching me.

He is indeed the God who cares. He is not an absent God, but a God who is present in our lives and cares about every detail. He sees our situations, and he does not turn his eyes away. "You are the God who sees me" (Genesis 16:13). He is the God who sees me. He is the God who sees you!

11

IT'S THE HORSE SENSE
OF THE MAN

A WORD FROM CHRIS

I knew I needed to immediately seek counseling. A dear friend of mine urged me to try the counseling center at his church. I did, and that is when I met Jeff. Jeff has been a godsend and has done more to help us than could ever be imagined. He began to work with me and to walk with me, serving as God's hands and feet to help heal our family. We praise the Lord for Jeff. He was another one of the many miracles that God poured out on our marriage.

A GOOD FRIEND of Chris's pointed him in the direction of a great Christian counseling center, and that is where we met Jeff. Chris went on July 5, and right away Jeff began to help him process the issues at hand and to direct Chris down the path to healing. Chris confessed everything to Jeff. This was not Jeff's first rodeo concerning this issue. Jeff was well versed in how to help Chris, and he embraced all that Jeff was telling him and began putting these concepts into practice. I saw the wonderful fruit that was occurring in Chris's counseling sessions with Jeff. This was vital to our healing process, and I began meeting with Jeff also. Sometimes we went separately, sometimes together. Either way, we never left without great progress toward our healing. Jeff showed us the power of God's grace that could heal us.

After my first individual visit with Jeff, I was thrilled. I knew that he could help us. I could see why Chris was making such great strides and looking forward to each visit. There are many excellent counselors, but Jeff was the one God chose for us, so he was a perfect fit. I texted Chris a quote from my favorite movie, *What About Bob.* After Bob's first visit with his psychiatrist, Bob told him, "Dr. Marvin, you can help me. For the first time in my life, I feel like there's hope." There was hope for us. There was help for us.

We had tried to fix our marriage over the past four years on our own without counseling. Now I understand the error of our thinking. For us, Godly counsel was an absolute necessity to the healing of our marriage. It would be beneficial in the healing of any marriage. There were four key factors that contributed to the healing of our marriage.

- God was at work. This was all being orchestrated by God. Our hearts just needed to be soft, receptive, and obedient.

- The God-given wise counsel of Jeff was vital, directing us in the way to individual healing and the restoration of our marriage.

- Chris had a repentant heart and was doing all he knew to make progress toward a deeper relationship with God and the healing of our marriage. He had developed a pattern of feeding his stronghold for a long time. But our God is able to pull down strongholds in our life.

- We realized that both sides of the fence in our marriage needed work. Major surgery was needed for each of us. The Great Surgeon made it clear that he was performing a double heart transplant.

As all of these factors came into play, God gave me a perfect peace, in fact a command, to continue to strive for the restoration of our marriage. If anyone is truly willing to make a marriage work, no one should stand in the way, including a spouse. The enemy tried many times to foil our reconciliation, but God continued to put his stamp of approval on this process. This gave us the gumption to press on.

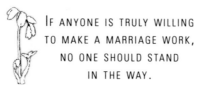

IF ANYONE IS TRULY WILLING
TO MAKE A MARRIAGE WORK,
NO ONE SHOULD STAND
IN THE WAY.

It seemed that God was healing us at an incredible rate. To some, it may seem unimaginable that we embraced God's healing so quickly, but for me it had been well over four years, and prayers were finally being answered. I told Jeff one day that I knew we would be restored and I didn't want to waste any time by trying to make it difficult. I was ready for business. Chris told me at one point that he wanted to have a great marriage again. I told him I didn't want great. I wanted amazing.

Healing hearts and restoring broken things are God's specialty. Still, it seemed quite miraculous to me that my own heart was mending and being restored like new. My love for Chris grew even greater than it had been before. We were not finished with our journey of healing. We had some very difficult times ahead. But any journey worth taking is worth investing in. If something is worthwhile, it's worth taking a while. This journey required a vital ingredient: time. God designed it that way because through the passage of time, we learn a new concept, process it, and make it our own. Then we repeat these same steps with the next thing that God is teaching us. The journey was good. I embraced it and looked forward to each new thing that God had in store for us.

IF SOMETHING IS WORTHWHILE, IT'S WORTH TAKING A WHILE.

God's healing continued to bring gifts of newness. It was like I had a new husband, or at least a new and improved one. He was returning to the vibrant love he had once had for God. Yet this love was brand new. We began putting new Christian artwork all over the house so that Scriptures engulfed us. We changed several things in our home because we were making a fresh start. We had a new church and enjoyed our long drive there each week. My husband was wearing a new wedding ring that God told him to buy. Eventually, I got a new wedding band also. God was renewing every aspect of our life. "Behold, I am making all things new" (Revelation 21:5, ESV).

Over and over, God showed me that he is the God of "re-"! What a prefix that is. The prefix *re-* means to do again or to return to its original state. The only time God needs to do something again is when we have messed up his original plan. But when God does something again, he can make it better than it was before. He is the Redeemer, Refiner, Restorer, Rebuilder, Refresher, Reconciler, Regenerator, and Repairer. The list goes on. You can probably think of twenty more. He was all of those things to us and many more. For any name of God I could think of, he was that to us. Praise to the God of "re-."

12

WHATEVER

SO I WILL VERY GLADLY SPEND
FOR YOU EVERYTHING I HAVE AND
EXPEND MYSELF AS WELL.

2 CORINTHIANS 12:15

HEALING FROM THIS type of betrayal is not easy. Trust me. Although I desired complete healing for both of us, the road was long and winding. It was painful. But I am a firm believer, now more than ever, that we are refined into Christ's likeness through trials. We must have our foundation set on Jesus Christ if we are going to make it through the difficulties in our lives.

After Job lost almost everything he would call a blessing in his life, he said in Job 1:21 (ESV), "The Lord gave and the Lord has taken away; blessed be the name of the Lord." Some translations add in the words *praise* or *worship the Lord*. Imagine saying that after you had lost your entire livelihood and all of your children! Was this Job for real? Yes, he was real. It would be challenging for a person to say those words on the latter side of a trial, but even more of a challenge to say those words while in the midst of trials, before restoration or resolution. Job said them when everything was taken away and nothing had been restored to him yet. But sometimes that is the only time we will say it, because that is when God is all we have, and we are finally in complete surrender to him.

I have tried to get in the habit of saying in my heart "whatever." It's not an indifferent kind of "whatever," but more of a prayer of surrender. I pray that to God when I basically want to say, "Whatever you want in my life, I am willing." I want that to always be the desire of my heart, though it does not always manifest itself in pure obedience. My prayer is something like, "Lord, I am yours, do with me what you want. Whatever. If you say I am to come home to be with you today, I am ready. Whatever. If you say I am to stay here and walk through fires with you, I am willing. Whatever." It is my simple means of trying to express that I only want his will and nothing else. Nothing else matters. My heart desires to always have that attitude. I am quite imperfect at it, yet I will continue to try. Whatever, God.

Trials have a way of bringing you close to God or pushing you further away. I had been brought close to God. Very close. In the past, I had known he was always with me, but as with anyone, sometimes we can get in the routine of life, and we may not always sense his heavy presence. But for me, going through this trial with Chris, it was as if God was closer and more real than if he had been standing beside me physically. During the few years that preceded this event, when things were getting tough, I had moments of extreme closeness with God. Other times, it seemed like there were moments of great distance because I was not seeing the results I desired. I was wondering where God was. But since that first week when God rattled Chris's cage and God told me to "watch this," there has not been a speck of doubt about God's care for me, not an instance of feeling outside of his presence, not an inkling of wondering if he was in control. It was out of my control. It always had been, but now I knew it. God had this thing. This was God's show, and I was sure of it.

Several weeks after Chris moved out, I was with some of my close friends. We were talking about my current situation. One of them genuinely and lovingly said, "I am so sorry that you have to go through this." And she was truly sorry about it.

I have said similar things to friends in tough spots. I so appreciated those kind words. Those were good and tender words. But I had to honestly reply, "I am not sorry. God is doing a mighty work. If this is what it took to bring Chris around, I will go through it. Whatever. I will fight any battle God sends my way. I will go anywhere God says to go. Wherever. I will walk through a fire with him." And the crazy thing was, I meant it. But that kind of resolve, "*whatever*" resolve, is something that God places in us. It is not of me. It is from God alone. Walking through a fire with God is the most glorious place to be. I would rather walk through a fire with God than through the most comfortable imaginations of my heart without him.

The conversation with my friends then turned to the realization that the enemy will target anyone who is trying to walk with God. This group of friends did seem to be going through a more than generous share of spiritual warfare at the time. Soon after, I received this text from a friend who had been a part of the conversation: "This is from my Bible study lesson this week: 'A person has hardly begun to have a real fight on her hands until she starts serving in her full throttle giftedness and effectiveness. She who proves a threat earns an enemy you bet will do everything he can to make her sorry.'"[6] My friend texted further, "Thanks for not being sorry and continuing to fight the battle."

Whoa, I had said I was not sorry that I was in this situation, but this quote said that Satan wants to make me sorry. But I responded in confidence. My text message reply was: "Thank you. I say, 'Satan, bring it. You will be sorry. I will never be sorry that I serve the King of Kings. My God will devour you!' Satan prowls around like a lion looking for whom he may devour. But he is not the Lion. He just tries to be like the true, mighty Lion, the Lion of the Tribe of Judah who conquers all. Jesus is roaring for my family" (1 Peter 5:8, Revelation 5:5).

You may think my response presumptuous, but I responded with confidence because I know that God is more than able to handle anything the wicked devil sends my way. We are overcomers by the blood of the Lamb, and Satan is the defeated foe. Romans 8 says, "What shall we say to these things? If God is for us, who can be against us? No, in all these things we are more than conquerors through him who loved us." (v. 31, 37, ESV)

My friend responded with several more texts, but finished with the most wonderful words that, unbeknownst to her, were from a passage that Chris and I had been claiming. "The best part about Job's story is 42:12, 'The Lord blessed the latter part of Job's life more than the former part.' You and Chris can cling to that promise for your marriage. Love you both."

I do cling to that promise. Many times, trials are self inflicted, brought on by our own poor choices. Sometimes they are due to the evils in this world. Some are tests that will show us what we are made of. No matter the origin, we can embrace them when we walk through the fire with God. We can trust that he is faithful to us throughout, and when we come out of that fire, we will be refined into a closer image of his son, Jesus Christ. That ongoing transformation in our hearts always makes the latter part of our life more blessed than the former. We can say *whatever* with confidence and anticipation.

13

FORGET ABOUT IT

Brothers, I do not consider myself
yet to have taken hold of it. But one
thing I do: Forgetting what is behind
and straining toward what is ahead,
I press on toward the goal to win
the prize for which God has called
me heavenward in Christ Jesus.

Philippians 3:13-14

THE BOOK OF Isaiah is a goldmine of encouragement.
Well, when you pull out selected verses, it can be. The book
of Isaiah demonstrates the true condition of man, that man
continually seeks to please himself and mock God. Isaiah
is full of judgments and anger and destruction. Will we
ever get it? Not fully, I'm sure. But nestled in between all
of those rough verses are some of the most beautiful songs
and poetry and snippets of truth that I have ever seen. And
how appropriate. God knows our sinfulness, knows that
judgment is needed, and knows that when we repent, we

need to be encouraged. In the midst of all of these harsh words is *grace*. When do we need it more than when we are in the pit? He wants to encourage us. He wants to be merciful.

I have always had my handpicked favorite verses from Isaiah. My list is long. They are my go-to verses for a pick-me-up, for strength, or for lifting a friend's load. My most favorite passage would probably be Isaiah 43, or least parts of it. It shares the lengths to which God is willing to go in order to rescue and reclaim his people. Isaiah 43:1–3 says:

> *But now, this is what the* LORD *says—he who created you, O Jacob, he who formed you, O Israel: "Fear not, for I have redeemed you; I have summoned you by name; you are mine. When you pass through the waters, I will be with you; and when you pass through the rivers, they will not sweep over you. When you walk through the fire, you will not be burned; the flames will not set you ablaze.*

God has redeemed me, and God calls me by name. That is unbelievable. I am his, and he walks through fires with me! And he will do the same for you. Overwhelming.

Further in this powerful chapter, we read Isaiah 43:18–19. "Forget the former things; do not dwell in the past. See, I am doing a new thing! Now it springs up; do you not perceive it? I am making a way in the desert and streams in the wasteland." Wow. Absolutely beautiful verses. God certainly wants us to move past our past. He wants to turn our wasteland into vibrant places where healthy streams can water it.

I had the privilege of teaching a lesson on these verses to a group of women in my Bible study. My focus for the teaching was to bring hope to people, no matter what had happened in their past. God doesn't want us to dwell on the past. Sure, we can learn from it. God absolutely wants us to learn from our mistakes and also find encouragement from the lessons of our past. In fact, God himself pointed to the many things he had done several times in this chapter. In verse 1, he reminded Israel that he created them, redeemed them, and summoned them. In verse 10, he said that he chose them. In verse 12, he told them that he revealed, saved, and proclaimed. In verse 16, he reminded them that he made a way for them to come out of Egypt through the sea. Yes, God refers to the past. In verse 26, he actually says to look at and review the past. He wants us to learn from it. But what he says not to do in verse 18 is *dwell* on it.

Dwell means to fasten one's attention to something. To let it consume us. To dwell on the past can paralyze us and keep us from moving forward. God has a big future for us, and we need to be free to move into that. His big plans include doing new things in our lives and using us in new ways. And he will do it in the midst of our desert wasteland. He says that he will make a way—right smack dab through the middle of the desert. The place where there is no life. He will make a stream through the wasteland.

The wasteland is a stagnant place of death. But a stream brings life and a fresh hope. That is what God was saying he would do for them. But the condition? Leave the past in the past. Forget the former things. Don't keep bringing it up to bring yourself down. Isaiah 43:20–21 reiterates that he is bringing a stream into their life, and that he wants to give a drink to his chosen people. A drink from God is a perfect drink that will never leave us thirsty again. It is a drink that would quench any thirst. We would no longer be thirsty for our own pleasures. Nor for the world's pleasures. Only for him. What is his motivation for this? He says the motivation is "that they might declare my praise" (Isaiah 43:21, ESV).

I love this passage. What a powerful truth! But the Lord began challenging me on who the message was for. Was it for the Bible study that I belonged to? Was it for me? Or was it for the whole world? Who needed to leave their past in the past so they could have a great future? Well, everyone did, I thought. The Lord prompted me with questions about who else I might be called to give this message to. Who did I know that needed to leave their past in the past and move forward with God? No question about it, he was speaking to me about sharing this passage with one of the women Chris had an affair with.

God showed me an inconsistency in my life: if I could stand up and tell a group of people that they should leave their past in the past and move forward with God, I could not in good conscience harbor in my heart that he should only do it for certain people. I knew he would do it for all people, no matter their connection with me. If I wanted to say, "God can do this for anyone," and then not want God to do it for some, I was a sick hypocrite who had her own agenda. I didn't want my own agenda. I wanted God's agenda. I wanted what he wanted. Restoration for all.

I had told God at the beginning of this journey that I would walk through any fire with him. Well, here came an opportunity. Was I willing to walk through it with him? I could claim Isaiah 43:2, "When you pass through the waters, I will be with you; and when you pass through the rivers, they will not sweep over you. When you walk through the fire, you will not be burned; the flames will not set you ablaze." God was with me, so I was willing.

I had been through this similar fire before with the other affairs, but God told me to travel it again. I asked God for strength and perfect timing. At this point, we were seven weeks out from this affair being brought to light. God had been doing such a mighty work in my heart, yet it was still very fresh. I had already forgiven her, and told her that through a text message, but now I felt I needed to express it face to face. A person in that situation may hear someone express forgiveness, but they do not always receive or believe it. It just seems too impossible. She was hurting. She was well aware of her sin and was trying to piece back her life. I did not need to remind her she had sinned, but I wanted her to have hope. Hope that there could be a life-giving stream in the midst of the desert.

I contacted the woman and her husband, and made an appointment to meet with them. As I drove there, the song "Forgiveness" by Matthew West came on the radio. The song was inspired by the true story of a mother who forgave the drunk driver who took her daughter's life in a car accident. This song confirmed why I was doing what I was doing. I had heard an interview about this song previously, which spoke about what a difference the forgiveness had made in the life of the man who had made this huge mistake. The forgiveness allowed him to move forward. People forgive great offenses all the time. It is by God's grace that we can do that. Who am I to not forgive? Am I in the place of God? And beyond that, who am I to not want someone to be restored to God. That is what he wants, and so I do too.

WHO AM I NOT TO FORGIVE?

God placed in my heart a great forgiveness and compassion on that day. Our ability to forgive and express it is supernatural. I met with the woman and her husband, and I expressed my forgiveness in person. I could see her heart melt in her facial expression. I had no bitter feelings toward her. We were simply two sinners whose sins had been covered by the blood of Jesus. We shared and cried and embraced. I shared that I only wanted the best for her family and that I would continue to pray for them. I also shared Isaiah 43:18–19. I told her that God could really do this. He really could make a way in the desert and put streams in the wasteland. God is so good and works in ways we can't predict because he used this couple to give me hope also. Our meeting was another of God's miracles. I left their home blessed because they also shared tender thoughts with me. God showed up that day in a mighty way. God can do what man says can't be done.

It may have been easier for me because of her humble attitude and words of sorrow. I know that this is not always the case when we attempt to share our forgiveness with people. I can't answer for all of those stories, but I know that God can place it in hearts to forgive. How he does it is his business.

What I initially thought would be a very difficult meeting turned into quite a blessing. Simply being present while God did a miraculous work was a privilege. It was not about me, but about the healing of hearts. Since God went before me, he made the way. He made the way in the desert and the stream in the wasteland. The very verses that prompted me to pursue the meeting for the sake of someone else ended up ministering to me. He turned the tables and blessed me. That's our God.

14

THERE'S NO CONDEMNATION IN THIS HOUSE, BROTHER

JESUS STRAIGHTENED UP AND ASKED
HER, "WOMAN, WHERE ARE THEY?
HAS NO ONE CONDEMNED YOU?"

"NO ONE, SIR," SHE SAID. "THEN NEITHER
DO I CONDEMN YOU," JESUS DECLARED.
"GO NOW AND LEAVE YOUR LIFE OF SIN."
JOHN 8:10-11

AS TIME PROGRESSED and God continued to strengthen us, we began the long journey of attempting to make things right with so many people who had been hurt by the affairs. Honestly, at first, it was all we could do to keep our own heads above water. But the time had come. We felt that God was urging us to move forward with helping others heal. Chris had so much guilt from his actions. It took a lot to muster up the confidence to face those whom he had hurt. These efforts would certainly not change the facts or the consequences, but trying to make amends was in order. There can be much healing when people are honest with each other. When a contrite sinner repents, hearts can melt into forgiveness.

Chris and I worked together on this. We are one, and we were unified in this endeavor. We had a long list of people with whom we wanted to share our story and beg forgiveness. There is no secret ingredient or a single, correct way to reach out to people. Everyone seemed to have their own way to deal with this circumstance, and we learned so much about being sensitive to what people need and what they are ready for. It was hard to know how to approach each person, but through it all, Chris kept his resolve to attempt to connect with everyone we felt we hurt the most.

While most of the contacts bore fruit, sometimes we were met with coldness. We could understand this, since the hurt was so deep. This particular sin comes with many consequences, and one of them is the loss of relationships, either temporarily or permanently.

There were several different scenarios with how each individual reacted to us.

- Some people were willing to forgive.

- Some were unwilling to forgive at that moment, but were willing to try to achieve a place of forgiveness as time passed.

- Others had no intention of ever forgiving.

Even within each of these scenarios, other factors come into play. Sometimes a person is able to forgive but is not capable of continuing a relationship any longer. I say that without judgment but as a reality that I have come to know. Maybe enough time just hasn't passed. It is hard to pinpoint how much time is enough to be able to feel like a relationship can resume.

Sometimes when forgiveness is absent, it is because the forgiveness is conditional—waiting to see if there has been true repentance. That is a very difficult thing to discern about another person's heart. This is made even more difficult when there is no communication between the two parties. I also understand this reaction, and I am learning to allow others the necessary time to go through this difficult process of forgiveness, which I also had to do.

Personally, I believe that true forgiveness is unconditional. We may not feel that the offender deserves to be forgiven, but in truth, no one deserves forgiveness. I'm overjoyed that Jesus didn't wait for me to deserve to be forgiven before he forgave me. Otherwise, he would still be waiting. I would still be waiting. We would all still be waiting. Author Lewis B. Smedes puts it into perspective, "To forgive is to set a prisoner free and discover that the prisoner was you."

This process began within the first couple of months by speaking to people as they came across our path. Many folks contacted us to see how we were doing and to ask if they could help. Chris was able to share with them how God was cleaning him up and the surgical work God was doing in our marriage. Chris was also able to share with several members and leaders of our new church about the road we had travelled. They also contributed to our healing, which still continues today.

It was a privilege to be able to give God the glory and share the testimony of changed lives. We had covered things up for so long, it was refreshing to hear Chris tell and retell the story without holding back the truth of the depth of his sin. He spoke about it to almost everyone he came in contact with. Chris declared outright to so many people that he had been in the depths of deep sin and that with God's help, he was turning his back on that life.

We continued to make our list and attempted to get to everyone we could think of that may have been hurting over this situation. We made our way through contacts with dozens of people. At one point, Jeff, our counselor, gently told us that he felt we had done enough. He said he could see that we had made a strong effort. He also encouraged us by letting us know that, though we genuinely wanted to make things right, it just wouldn't or couldn't happen for everyone. There are some bridges, we would learn, that may remain burned.

Each encounter brought us further in our healing. Each encounter taught us a new lesson. Yet, we have come to realize that overall, the soft answers helped us the most. I've heard our pastor say, "Grace is the greater motivator." I am aware that many times, hard words need to be spoken. I agree that as we deal with biblical truths, we need to uphold high standards. I also believe the delivery of the truth needs to be coupled with grace. Chris wrestled with the fact that he had not been good at this in the past, having had a black-and-white attitude with little leeway for grace and opinions other than his own. But we learned that it is possible, even necessary, to stand on the truth and be gracious at the same time. God had a plan to restore our marriage, but he also made it clear that we needed to learn a few things about graciously caring for other people.

Our ordeal taught us how much grace we needed, and that so many hurting people hunger for grace. We all need grace lavished on us from God as well as grace from others. We also realized that we, after our great trial, had more grace and love to hand out. Luke 7:36–50 tells of a sinful woman who humbly and tearfully washed Jesus' feet. Others who were present were disgusted by Jesus' acceptance of her. They didn't understand how Jesus would accept such a *dirty* person. They could not comprehend why he would be interested in her, or why the woman would be so desperately longing for a connection with Jesus.

Jesus used the opportunity to tell a parable to beautifully explain that a person who has been forgiven a great debt can become more grateful and tender. Jesus began by posing a question in Luke 7:41–43, "'Two men owed money to a certain moneylender. One owed him five hundred denarii, and the other fifty. Neither of them had the money to pay him back, so he canceled the debts of both. Now which of them will love him more?' Simon replied, 'I suppose the one who had the bigger debt canceled.' 'You have judged correctly,' Jesus said."

Later in the passage, Jesus explained that this translates into our spiritual lives. When we have sinned much and incur great *debt*, we need much forgiveness. When we repent and are forgiven, our natural reaction is to love the one who forgives. It changes us. It heals the debt by removing its burden. This is how the woman felt for Jesus. Luke 7:47a

(ESV) states, "Therefore I tell you, her sins, which are many, are forgiven—for she loved much."

He also taught that the contrary is true. Luke 7:47b (ESV) states, "But he who is forgiven little, loves little." We saw that lesson become evident in our own lives. Prior to this, we did not fully realize the magnitude of how much we needed to be forgiven and exactly how much Jesus had paid to forgive us. We were measuring by human standards the various degrees of sin. Up to this point in our lives, we did not feel we had committed a *big* sin. But then it sank in: every sin is big in the eyes of God. When we got a glimpse of how much forgiveness we needed, it heightened our appreciation for the one who forgave us. As a result, we want to forgive and love others so much more. God truly changed us, and we have a greater compassion for people who are hurting. We will not be perfect at this, but we certainly want God to help us get better at it. We don't want to "love little".

We had several encounters that are dear to our hearts. But some of the most tender moments were with my own family. We met with my mom and two of my sisters and brothers-in-law who live nearby. At each stop, we had some anxiety and much anticipation of how things would turn out. This was indeed a sensitive topic and hard conversations took place. But at every stop, after we each had the opportunity to express our feelings and say our piece, grace was given. Awesome, marvelous, incredible, unbelievable, amazing grace.

One of the beautiful things about these meetings with family was that, once the issue had been brought out in the open, the matter was not brought up again. Maybe we learned that from my dad. That is the way my dad acted toward me when I told him I was pregnant out of wedlock twenty-six years before these meetings. He never brought the matter up again. I knew I had sinned. There was no need to leave me in the pit. And now, Chris knew he had sinned. My family was not going to leave him in the pit. Chris has told me he knew that if my dad had been alive at this time, he too would have spoken his mind and then been our number one cheerleader. He would have shown us grace.

Our next hurdle to tackle was my oldest sister, Tina, and her husband, John. They lived four hours away. We had been hearing a lot of talk that John was upset. Of course he was upset. Everyone was upset. There had been much talk about how John would react to Chris. We were warned to take cover. This seemed uncharacteristic to me, yet we had never faced anything of this magnitude. Among the brothers-in-law, John had been in the family the longest and had sort of become the "patriarch" since my dad had died. With these fears in our hearts, we began the trip to their home, knowing that whatever the outcome, this had to be done.

We arrived at their home after the long drive and took a deep breath. Tina met us first at the door and hugged us both. That made Chris feel more at ease, but we expected that from Tina. As we moved farther into the house, John hugged me, as usual. John and I were always solid. But John was quick to move past me and seemed preoccupied with getting to Chris. It was urgent. He had something on his heart, and it needed to be addressed. John grabbed Chris. He hugged him hard and said, "There is no condemnation in this house, brother." Chris began to weep. God's grace was pouring out all over him again. There was such a need for grace, and it just wouldn't stop coming. What a blessing from God.

We sat with Tina and John for dinner, and two of their adult kids who were home that evening joined us. Prayer started our time. We talked with them for quite a while, and thoughtful questions were posed. Good insight was given. Love was shared. There have been so many highlights and lowlights throughout our journey. This was one of the best times. It was a time anointed by God. To us, this home was another place of holy ground.

There was great relief getting this particular set of meetings over. It meant the world to me to know that our family was with us in this. They were not on my side, and they were not on Chris's side. They were on the side of our marriage. Over the next few weeks, we felt as if we had come to a close in reaching out to everyone we felt we needed to at that time. God kept finishing tasks and moving us to the next step. What did he have in store for us next? It just kept getting more and more exciting as we watched the show he was orchestrating.

15

HOLD ME UNDER

A WORD FROM CHRIS

*As God continued to work in our lives, he led me to
want to be baptized again. My wife baptized me
on September 16, 2012.*

SINCE THE BEGINNING of this journey, Chris had a
tender connection with God. He continued to journal and
study and fill himself with things of God. He asked me to
fill his iPod© portable music device with Christian music.
It was fun to surprise him with new songs that I loved,
and he now loved them all too. He loved the lyrics and
would continue to text them to me throughout the day. He
loved everything that God was putting before him. He was
a sponge soaking up all of God. He reminded me of a new
believer, and I was smiling to God the whole time. When
I originally told God that I was watching to see what God
would do in this situation, it was, sadly, a challenge to God
that was meant to put God on the spot. At that time, I
honestly didn't think God was going to put on much of a

show. But this was the best show I had ever seen, and it was in my face. God turned the tables on me. "If you want to see a show, I can perform!" Boom!

One morning during the painful years prior to our time of healing, I awoke in the morning to a song playing on the radio. It was "Heal Me" by Aaron Jeoffrey. It talks about being numb to God, and the singer cries out for God to heal his mind, heart, and eyes. At that time, I prayed that song over Chris, sadly reminiscing that at one time he had a deep, vibrant relationship with God that was now gone. I wanted that back for his sake and also for my sake. It was a selfless prayer, I thought, to lift up my husband to the Lord on this issue. I would often, with pride, say to God that I wasn't pointing a finger at Chris. After all, I did admit once that I was imperfect too. But I thought God needed to know that Chris was really the one who needed help.

Years later, after Chris and I were on this journey of healing, God saw fit that I would hear that song again. We had already been through much soul searching when, suddenly, it hit me in the face that the lyrics to the song were about me. How had I been so blind? I was the one who had become somewhat numb toward God. Me. I was the one who needed my mind, heart, and eyes to be healed. I had been pointing at Chris all that time, when all along it was me. My faith had become circumstantial. If my life was going good, God was good. If my life filled with turmoil, God's presence was questionable. I realized the challenge in my spirit was to acknowledge that God is God is God. No matter my circumstances. He is never changing and always faithful, even when I am not. God wanted me to see myself for what I was, a prideful wife who liked to point a finger.

God got my attention. It finally sank in. I saw that God was putting on a show in Chris's life, and he was changing me too. Thank you, God. I am a life that is changed forever.

I put the song "Heal Me" on Chris's iPod© and shared with him that it had been important to me during my painful years and also in our current situation. We often discussed the songs and Scriptures we came across. Later that day, I walked into his office, and he was listening to that song. He was weeping. His heart was broken again for all of the pain he had caused and the effect his actions had on my walk with God. Of course, I was responsible for how I reacted to God, but he could see that the circumstances of our injured marriage had challenged my faith. His heart was so soft toward God, and the things that grieved God also grieved him. He grieved over the pain I had endured.

This newfound softness led him to desire to be baptized again as a symbol of rededicating his life to Christ. Our salvation is solidified the moment we accept Christ as our Savior, admitting that we are sinners and believing that he is the only way to our Holy God. It is Jesus' blood shed on the cross that paid the price for our sins. A price that, if left unpaid, will keep us separated from God.

Baptism is an intentional act of obedience that is a public testimony of a person who has chosen to follow Christ. The old life is buried, and in Christ alone, we are raised to new life. New life. We were living a new life.

We scheduled the baptism. Chris was set on me baptizing him, and I was honored to do it. I was all in. We greatly anticipated this monumental day because it represented so much to us. It represented lives changed, a marriage saved, a family unified, and a God-sized story to be told. I was in awe of all that God had done, and I am amazed daily by his unmerited grace and interest in our lives. I can never say thank you enough to the King of kings who saved my marriage, changed my heart, and brought a dead man and woman back to life.

The day had arrived, and a wonderful staff helped us get into clothes they provided for the Baptism ceremony, including T-shirts with "Free" printed on the front. They attached a waterproof microphone to me and the others who would also be baptizing loved ones on that day. The staff gave all of us some words of instruction. They said we could say a personal, short sentence or two and then proceed with the script for baptism. What? Say something? I was so caught up in the experience Chris was gearing up for that I hadn't even thought that I would have to speak. I just planned on dunking him. Chris wondered if I would hold him under for a little extra time, just to make sure it took! I decided that I would just say what was on my heart at the moment of baptism, and hopefully not fumble my words enough to make it on the next episode of *America's Funniest Home Videos*. But this day wasn't about my words. It was about the souls who were in the baptismal pool that day starting a new life.

The moment arrived, and I was overjoyed to be a part of this great event.

"My name is Colleen McKain, and this is my husband Chris. I have had the privilege of watching God change a heart. Chris, because you have placed your faith and trust in Jesus Christ, I now baptize you in the name of the Father, Son, and Holy Spirit."

And I plunged him under the water. A cleansing flood washed over Chris, and he saw a new future before him. Praise the Lord. New life. Our children and their families came to the service, and an exclamation mark was placed on the progress of all God had been doing.

16

519 GIRL

A WORD FROM CHRIS

My wife Colleen is my "whoever" that is described in James 5:19–20: "My brothers and sisters, if one of you should wander from the truth and someone should bring that person back, remember this: Whoever turns a sinner from the error of their way will save them from death and cover over a multitude of sins." Colleen has helped save me from death and from a multitude of sins.

CHRIS HAD MANY special verses that ministered to him through the process of healing. One set of verses became especially meaningful to us both. To preface this, the work of salvation is Jesus' business. He is the only one with the power to save us. His Holy Spirit draws us in, and the blood of Jesus cleanses each individual thoroughly, so as to be made holy before the Father. But as relational beings, we also know that people make an impact as we walk through this life. Many times, we are changed through the efforts and actions of others, which is evidenced through our story in this book by the countless souls who helped us on our journey. Simply put, we need each other.

As stated above, James 5:19–20 says, "My brothers and sisters, if one of you should wander from the truth and someone should bring that person back, remember this: Whoever turns a sinner from the error of their way will save them from death and cover over a multitude of sins."

Chris claimed this verse for our marriage and his healing. He calls me his "519 girl" because, from his point of view, I was the person, the "whoever," who brought him back to the truth. These verses are so special to us that we had them burned on the leather of our freshly rebound Bibles. God has renewed us through this process, and now our Bibles are also new.

The entire passage surrounding those verses is quite applicable to our situation, which makes sense, because the context in which we find every verse is key to understanding it. Backing up to James 5:13–16, James is talking about people who are in trouble, sick, or weak. Both Chris and I had been troubled and weak many times through this process and in great need of prayer. And as James states, after prayer and confession, healing took place.

James 5:17–18 refers to Elijah, who had prayed earnestly for a drought, and subsequently it did not rain in Israel for three and a half years. Then, at the appointed time set by God, he prayed, and the heavens gave rain and the land produced crops again. It would be easy to look at these verses in James and take them only at face value and think that the only lesson here is about earnest prayer. Indeed, that is part of the lesson. But additionally, when we go back to the actual passage to which James is referring in 1 Kings 18, we see the context of Elijah's prayer.

Israel had been turning from God for generations, and even more so under the leadership of evil King Ahab, who led them in worship to a false god, Baal. A judgment was brought down on the land in the form of a drought. Yet God did not bring the drought to wipe his people out, but rather to bring them back to him. Many times in our lives, it is in the trials that we cry out to God even more. That was the ultimate goal of this trial: to bring the Israelites back to God. Near the end of the drought, Elijah said to Israel in 1 Kings 18:21, "How long will you waver between two opinions? If the LORD is God, follow him; but if Baal is god, follow him." Yes, the goal was for them to see God for who he was and return to him.

The story continues with a showdown between Baal and the One True Living God. Both had the opportunity to set a bull ablaze on an altar by their own power. Baal failed miserably, and neither smoke nor spark nor flame was ignited on the bull on his altar. Of course he failed. After all, he was a false, dead god. Then it was Elijah's turn to pray for our mighty God to start the fire on the altar. It says in 1 Kings 18:36–37:

> *At the time of sacrifice, the prophet Elijah stepped forward and prayed: "O Lord, God of Abraham, Isaac and Israel, let it be known today that you are God in Israel and that I am your servant and have done all these things at your command. Answer me, O Lord; answer me, so these people*

will know that you, O Lord, are God, and that
you are turning their hearts back again.

Again, this beautiful passage shows us that the main purpose for the drought was more than a judgment. It was to show Israel who God was and encourage them to return to him. And God showed up and showed off. In 1 Kings 18:38, we are told, "Then the fire of the Lord fell and burned up the sacrifice, the wood, the stones and the soil, and also licked up the water in the trench." What a display of power and victory.

This Old Testament passage about Elijah fits perfectly in the passage in James 5:13–20. The James passage began by referring to people who are in trouble and weak and in need of healing, just like the Israelites. The passage contains instructions to confess and go to prayer in order to find that healing, just what the Israelites needed to do. The passage shows that if someone brings back to the Lord one who has wandered from the truth, he will save him from death and cover a multitude of sins. This is just what Elijah did for the Israelites when he pursued them, in hopes that they would return to God. When Elijah built the altar with a bull on it and God rained down fire and consumed the offering completely, it proved that Jehovah was the One True Living God. The people could see who God was and return to him. We see that they got the message in 1 Kings 18:39: "When all the people saw this, they fell prostrate and cried, 'The Lord—he is God! The Lord—he is God!'"

Even though Israel had sinned grievously against the Lord, God never gave up on them. Their souls were at stake, and their souls were worth pursuing. God was willing to do whatever it took to win them back. Elijah was used by God, as his spokesman, to draw them back. This can be a perfect parallel to our lives, for we are all wanderers who turn from God at times. We need God to woo us back, and sometimes he uses others to do it.

God never stopped pursuing the souls in Israel. God never stopped pursuing Chris's soul. God never stopped pursuing my soul. And he will not stop pursuing yours either.

May we never stop allowing God to use us as he did Elijah, to pursue straying souls.

Again, James 5:19–20 states, "My brothers and sisters, if one of you should wander from the truth and someone should bring that person back, remember this: Whoever turns a sinner from the error of their way will save them from death and cover over a multitude of sins." This is God's will. It is stated beautifully in 2 Peter 3:9, "He is patient with you, not wanting anyone to perish, but everyone to come to repentance."

17

THERE'S JUST LIFE

I PROCLAIM RIGHTEOUSNESS IN THE GREAT
ASSEMBLY; I DO NOT SEAL MY LIPS,
AS YOU KNOW, O LORD.

I DO NOT HIDE YOUR RIGHTEOUSNESS
IN MY HEART; I SPEAK OF YOUR
FAITHFULNESS AND SALVATION.

I DO NOT CONCEAL YOUR LOVE AND YOUR
TRUTH FROM THE GREAT ASSEMBLY.

PSALM 40:9–10

IN WHAT SEEMS like such a long time ago, I had told
God that I was watching. I was watching to see what he
would and could do in this seemingly hopeless situation
in my life. I even doubted that he could perform. And
thankfully, because our God is more than able, he put on
a magnificent show. He performed heart surgery on both
Chris and me. And if we will allow him, he will continue to
do maintenance on our hearts daily.

Heart maintenance really does need to be a daily discipline. God has brought us a long way, but until we go home to see Jesus, we are not finished. He has much more to complete in us. We are far from perfect. We do not know what the future holds, but I am sure that we will stumble and fall along the way. We will need to completely rely on God to get us through. There will certainly be more trials in this life that come our way. But entering each trial with God by our side makes our path in life full of hope rather than fear.

Our counselor described a dramatic scene to Chris at one of his first visits. He described a forest which was beautiful and strong and vibrant. It was a picture of what a forest should look like. Yet in a sudden moment, a spark ignited in the forest. At first, it was just that, a spark. But soon, as sparks tend to do when paired with fuel, fire broke out. It grew and grew until it was a full-blown forest fire. A blazing inferno.

It continued to burn until all of what had once been so beautiful was completely destroyed, or so it seemed.

One could look at the devastated area and proclaim that ruin had come. Not a tree was left standing. Not a green twig remained. Even the animals that once received their sustenance from the forest were gone. The forest was dead and deserted.

In time, however, a small bit of new growth appeared. You see, there were roots below the ground and seeds that had not been destroyed. The forest was still alive, even though by all appearances, it looked completely dead. As the seasons passed, the forest became verdant once again, and there was no leashing its resolve. The remains of the fire left rich nutrients on the forest floor. The new growth was good and healthy and robust. The forest became stronger than before, since the weak and diseased plants and trees had now been cleaned out.

Our counselor described this as a parallel to Chris's life and, eventually, to our marriage. What seemed to be a total loss was, in reality, a total cleaning out of a damaged and diseased lifestyle of sin. It was a necessary fire to bring our forest into wholeness and health. It was a fire that had to burn. And we had the privilege—yes, the privilege—to walk through it. On the other side, there was evidence of the fire, but the outcome was miraculous. What had been left for dead continued to live. And live vigorously.

The destruction was a reality for the forest. The destruction was a reality in our marriage. The pain was a reality. The consequences were a reality. Even still, I wouldn't trade it for the world. Somehow through the wreckage, we found out that God was "able to do immeasurably more than all we ask or imagine" (Ephesians 3:20).

If given a choice, I would not go back to my life before this journey of allowing God to have his way in my life as never before. A. W. Tozer is quoted as saying, "It is doubtful that God uses anyone significantly until he has hurt them deeply." One may find fault in this quote concerning where our pain originates, but setting that aside, if our pain and experiences bring us to a place in which God can use us more fully, bring it on.

I know some things to be true. Our world is broken. People need grace—loads of it. Multitudes are hurting everywhere. Many times we are ill-equipped to help hurting people. Jesus is the only answer for these sad but true situations. And he is so good at being the answer. It comes naturally for him. In fact, he was born for it.

PEOPLE NEED GRACE
—LOADS OF IT.

At one time, Chris and I had been fighting against each other. God showed us that we were not each other's enemies. We were on the same team. He showed us who the true enemy was and that we needed to fight the enemy together. So the tide turned. We began fighting for each other. We fought for our marriage. We fought for God's plan to prevail.

Every situation does not have the same beginnings. Every situation will not have the same end. The details of the middle are quite different. In addition to God's intervention, we found in our circumstance some of the elements that promoted our healing were: repentance, two softening hearts, and a willingness to change. Our supportive counselor and our family and friends were also vital. Sometimes, and maybe in your case, some or all of these positive elements might be absent. Both parties may not want to restore, repentance may be missing, or there may simply be no resolve to make it work. You may even have some people giving you conflicting advice about what to do next. But no matter where you find yourself, God will walk through it with you. A friend of mine once said, "I came to a point: if everything were taken away, God would be enough for me." No matter what is happening in your life, God is enough.

As I reflect on my life, I realize that I have learned more about life in these four years than all the others combined. This new understanding of life reminds me of a scene from the 1993 movie *Tombstone*. It is the story of the lives of two men, Wyatt Earp and Doc Holiday, trying to live life in the harshness of the Wild West. The scene is set in a sanatorium as Doc Holiday is living the last few moments of his life. He's lying in the hospital bed when Wyatt Earp comes to visit him. Wyatt was Doc's only friend, and the only man who ever gave him hope.

As the scene plays, they are reminiscing about the shared experiences of their lives when Doc asks Wyatt a simple yet thought-provoking question. He asks, "Wyatt, what do you want?"

Wyatt quickly responds, as if he'd pondered this question before. "Just to live a normal life." Their life together had been filled with fighting, the loss of loved ones, addictions, divorce, broken family relationships, and now the soon-approaching loss of each other. Any of these seem familiar? After experiencing all of these things, of course Wyatt would want a normal life. Who wouldn't? Anything but what he had lived up to this point.

But Doc, in all of his dying wisdom, understood why Wyatt's response was not accurate. From the perspective of his death bed, Doc had come to realize one important life lesson. With that lesson in mind, he responded to his dear friend, "There is no normal life, Wyatt. There's just life."

Chris and I have gone through life. Some amazing life. Some hard life. Just life. But by the grace of God, he walked through all of it with us. He was with us during the forest fire and on the other side of it. He took our pain and brokenness and made our life HIS story. He can make your life HIS story—if you will let him. After all, it's his show.

NOTES

1   Wong, Scott, "Phoenix Rejects $10M Offer from Infidelity Web Site," The Arizona Republic, Feb. 02, 2010 (accessed April 14, 2014).

2   "NFL Stadium Offered $25 M to Promote Adultery," TMZ.com, 2010-05-30 (accessed April 14, 2014).

3   Leeker, O. & Carlozzi, A., "Effects of Sex, Sexual Orientation, Infidelity Expectations, and Love on Distress Related to Emotional and Sexual Infidelity," Journal of Marital and Family Therapy 40 (2014): 68-91, doi:10.1111/j.1752-0606.2012.00331.x.

4   Ibid.

5   Ibid.

6   Beth Moore, *James: Mercy Triumphs* (Nashville: Lifeway Christian Resources, 2011), 164.

IT'S HIS SHOW STUDY GUIDE

For individuals, couples and groups
or for use as a counseling tool

The IT'S HIS SHOW Study Guide offers in-depth, guided questions to help people further examine and grow in their individual relationships with God and others. A sample chapter is available online at www.itshisshow.com.

Study Guide: ISBN 978-09985592-3-0

Available Summer 2017 through the publisher, the authors, online or through your favorite bookseller or distributor.

Churches, non-profit organizations and counselors, contact Encourage Publishing for special pricing.

info@encouragebooks.com, 812.987.6148
www.encouragebooks.com

ENCOURAGE
PUBLISHING

Thank you for reading IT'S HIS SHOW. Your feedback is important to us. Would you take a moment and post a review on your favorite site?

Amazon.com * Goodreads.com
itshisshow.com * encouragebooks.com

CONTACT THE AUTHORS

Guest Speakers * Booksignings
Interviews * Retreats * Webinars

"As the key speaker at a Grace Heartland Church women's retreat, Colleen inspired us with her honest story of a failing marriage and encouraged us with her understanding of God, how He is faithful and full of grace. Colleen encouraged us to "press on," trust God, and allow Him to transform our broken relationships. After all, God's ways are always best - Philippians 3:12-14."

Nancy Kersh
Grace Heartland Church, Elizabethtown, Kentucky

"I asked Chris and Colleen to share their story in our Marriage Project Class, knowing already that it was one of great heartache and sin, and great redemption. They humbly told their story and placed the emphasis on the amazing power and grace of God who brought them out of such a dark place. They were able to share their story with courage and vulnerability, realness and candor in a way that deeply touched the hearts of those in the class. From the responses of the participants, they connected to Chris and Colleen in a significant way and left with an infusion of hope."

Don Delafield, LMFT, LPC
Counseling Minister
Southeast Christian Church, Louisville, Kentucky

Contact the McKains online at www.itshisshow.com or through the publisher, info@encouragebooks.com.